A STRANGE OCCUPATION

A personal account of life in the British Zone of occupied Germany after the 1939-45 war, set against the background of a country utterly devastated and undergoing the painful process of being reorganised by its conquerors.

Despite the, at times, confused and contradictory attitudes of the authorites, much was done by ordinary members of the Occupation Forces to help the German people back to normal civilized living.

This story does not dwell on the hardships but reveals the comic and often bizarre aspects of a unique period in our recent history.

A STRANGE OCCUPATION

Georgiana Melrose

ARTHUR H. STOCKWELL LTD.
Elms Court   Ilfracombe
Devon

Cover design by P.M. McMurtry

To Franz

Illustrations set between pages 64 & 65

For in and out, above, about, below

'Tis nothing but a magic shadow show

Played in a box whose candle is the sun

Round which we phantom figures come and go.

Omar Khayam

ISBN 0 7223 2200-3
Printed in Great Britain by
Arthur H. Stockwell Ltd.
Elms Court   Ilfracombe
Devon

Part 1

I picked up the jacket, recoiling from the musty smell, and put it on, tugging the sleeves down but they still reached only to about three inches above the wrists. Then I ran my hand along the back of my neck where the stiff collar chafed. After fastening the brass buttons I stepped into the skirt and drew it up, swivelling it around my waist, but whichever way I tried, it hung sagging just above the knees. I took a look at myself in the full-length mirror. Heavens, what a sight!

Downstairs my mother and sister with a few neighbours were having coffee and awaiting the highlight of the evening's entertainment, my appearance in the new uniform. I went down and as I entered, doing my best to imitate a slinky model mincing along the catwalk, they all burst out laughing.

Certainly the whole thing was absurd — an ordinary young housewife to be putting on uniform for the first time just a year after the end of the war when most people were happily exchanging theirs for a 'demob' suit.

On recruitment in the London Office, a clerk, after demanding my vital statistics, had taken a jacket off a heap of clothes piled on a trestle-table like jumble in the village hall, and flung it at me; at the next table someone did the same with a skirt.

That curious uniform was a hastily assembled outfit issued to the newly recruited women members of the CCG, (Control Commission for Germany), the organization which was to take over many of the duties being performed by the armed services

5

since the end of hostilities in 1945.

The jacket and skirt in contrasting shades of blue were made of a coarse material like thick serge, and they clashed horribly, which was hardly surprising as at the end of the war the jackets had been found surplus to the requirements of the Civil Defence, and the skirts had been thrown out by the Fire Service. Presumably it had occurred to a sharp brain in the Foreign Office that putting the tops and bottoms together would be a cheap solution to the problem of equipping the female recruits with a new uniform. White cotton shirts, with black ties discarded from the Wrens, and black woollen school-girl type stockings completed the outfit, together with a heavy dark blue overcoat, navy blue beret with gilt badge, and black lace-up shoes.

The CCG 'coat-of-arms' was on the right sleeve of the jacket, and the left shoulder bore a green flash informing a confused world of our status — Civ. Mil. Gov. A civilian military government struck me as being paradoxical, to say the least. However, that badge appeared to be a sign of split minds in the Foreign Office, unable to decide which breed we should belong to, finally settling for a combination of both, allotting us army ranks as well as civilian grades.

With the end of the war came redundancy, the loss of my job as personnel officer in a large aircraft factory in Southampton. The factory promptly changed over to the manufacture of sinks, baths and other domestic hardware. Being made redundant did not upset me, for the reason could hardly have been better. In any case the excitement and glamour involved in the making of aeroplanes from drawing-board to take-off would not have transferred easily to the production of mundane household articles. So the search for a new job began. Like many others, I had been widowed and was therefore as free as the Lone Ranger to ride off into the unknown. In the newspapers I had often noticed references to various mysterious organisations operating in Germany, known only by their initials . . . .UNNRA, ...NAAFI, ...WVS, ... CCG, ...FANNY, and so on. I wrote to the lot and even managed to get two interviews, but the outcome was the same, "Things are rather difficult in Germany at present, but we'll let you know." The rest was silence.

Still living at my parents' home, with bank balance and my husband's RAF £70 gratuity dwindling fast, worry set in. Going through the daily perusal of advertisements, I came across one requesting somebody with welfare experience to supervise a thousand GI brides encamped on Salisbury Plain awaiting shipment to the United States — quite a challenge! I sat down and wrote a letter of application. The very next day, fortunately perhaps for both me and the GI brides, a note arrived from the CCG HQ in London requesting me to go for an interview about a job in Germany.

On arrival at the house in Princes Gardens I was directed to a door at the end of a long corridor. As I hesitated a moment before knocking I could see it all — a large impersonal boardroom with earnest officials seated at a long table, each poring over a copy of my carefully documented life history. Would I on the evidence be a suitable person to take part in the occupation and rehabilitation of post-war Germany?

Taking a deep breath, I knocked.

"Come in!"

But instead of stepping into the nerve centre of the Control Commission for Germany, clearly I had gatecrashed the hide-out of an eccentric professor, utterly lost in some esoteric research, possibly into the secret of perpetual motion, or even perpetual inertia.

Standing disconsolately ankle deep in a sea of paper was a small elderly gentleman in a dark overcoat. Papers and files were bursting out of half-open drawers, piled feet high on tables and chairs, stacked on every available surface. He had a shovel in his hand.

"Can't get it to burn," he remarked mournfully, pointing the shovel in the direction of the tiny grate where a single timid flame was about to give up the struggle, "and there's no more coal."

When I'd explained my presence, he fumbled through an untidy heap of papers on the desk. "I'm terribly sorry, my dear, but your application form doesn't seem to be here. Are you sure you sent it in?" Without waiting for an answer he continued. "Now, was it Timber Control you applied for?"

Somewhat taken aback I said, "No, I wanted a job in Education."

"You mean in the re-education of the Germans?"

"Yes, I suppose so."

"I am afraid there are no more jobs in the Education Branch. We had a great many applicants."

"Well, what jobs are there?"

"Let me see . . . there are a few vacancies in Timber Control."

"What's that?" I enquired with a distinct lack of interest.

"It's the branch controlling timber. You see, everything is controlled and that means timber too," he said patiently.

I tried to visualize myself as a sort of lumberjack sweating it out in a dark German forest and, although by this time I was feeling less particular, that sort of work did seem to fall a little short of my life high ideals and aspirations.

"Surely there must be something more suitable for me?"

"There are a few vacancies for Billet Supervisors, Grade 4. The starting rank is warrant officer. Would you be prepared to accept such a post?"

Without further questioning I said I would. The most important thing was to get out to Germany. Once there I would look around to see how the land lay. It seemed impossible to find out anything here. Certainly Billet Supervisor didn't sound a very challenging job, but it was better than nothing.

Later I heard from other applicants that their papers too had been lost, and in desperation they had agreed to take jobs for which they regarded themselves as totally unfitted.

The elderly gentleman then invited me out to lunch, and my spirits rose at the mouth-watering prospect of a big unrationed meal in a West End restaurant, but sank as quickly when the vision faded into callous reality — a dreary self-service café in a dank basement just around the corner.

But at least now I had the prospect of a job. The old man had said there would be no further interviews. I should just go home and await instructions. He counselled patience, a quality that was wearing pretty thin.

In my letter of application I had stated that I could speak some German, which was far from the truth. I didn't know any German, but was confident that I could pick it up quickly. I imagined that anyone with a knowledge of the language would be snapped up and given a top job. Perhaps it was just as well that my papers had been lost. I might have been tested out by an examiner, and then the game would have been up. Now it was beginning to sink in that I had accepted a boring and undemanding job, yet it seemed to carry quite a high rank, warrant officer, and whatever happened the life could not fail to be exciting — an adventure — maybe the start of a new career, although not as a billet supervisor. I'd made up my mind about that!

The old man had told me I could sign on for one year, and this I decided to do. After that it would be possible to renew the contract year by year.

At that time the thought of spending even one year in a country of which I was totally ignorant, and where conditions would certainly be abnormal, seemed to me a very long time indeed.

Back home I broke the news to my mother and sister.

"I'm even starting as a warrant officer," I announced with pride.

"Jolly good dear," they said, clearly impressed.

After that, things moved unbearably slowly, or more accurately they did not move at all. I had decided to make solicitous enquiries about those thousand GI brides, and whether they were still coralled on Salisbury Plain, when I received a faded yellow form headed Control Office for Germany and Austria, and addressed to Mrs G. Melrose.

'Dear Sir,' it began. *'I have to inform you that we can offer you a post as LAU Supervisor Grade 4 (Billets) CCG (British Element) starting pay £4 14s. 0d. weekly / Foreign Service allowance £25.'* There followed a list of detailed instructions to report to the 'Processing Unit'.

What bureaucratic mind had thought up that nasty phraseology? The same sort of dehumanised mentality I supposed, as those who referred to us as 'Bods'. In the event 'processing' could not have been a more appropriate word. In single file we passed slowly along like half finished products on the assembly-line, being jabbed in the arm, handed bits of paper, permits, passes, forms and finally — oh joy — a real bonus, a wad of £30 in notes and 200 clothing coupons! These, we were informed, were to be used for the sole purpose of buying extra warm underclothing.

Several 'Bods' endowed with more natural cunning than the rest, promptly returned to the end of the line to be presented with another £30 and another 200 clothing coupons whether they got more jabs was never revealed. I heard one character remark that that was good enough for him, and he'd changed his mind about going to Germany! We were madly excited about the coupons. During the war they had been amongst our most precious possessions, although nearly all the clothes to be had in the shops were of the mass produced 'utility brand'. The coupons were often swapped for rationed items of food, and the men, usually with less interest in clothes, were willing to sell them outright for cash. Luckily for me, my brother-in-law before he entered a monastery, had sold me his complete ration book, having decided that a bottle of whisky would be a more valuable contribution to his monastic welfare.

Now we had no intention of wasting this marvellous gift on sensible vests and knickers — 'Passion Killers'! Anyway, we were being kitted out for Europe, not for a polar expedition. After a quick consultation, the less high principled among us rushed off to Knightsbridge where we had a field-day buying frivolous things unknown for years, cocktail dresses, evening shoes, diaphanous nighties, flimsy 'smalls' etc.

On 21st April 1946 my marching orders arrived. I was to be at Victoria Station wearing my uniform and bringing only one suitcase weighing not more than 66 lb, together with all the relevant documents, Military Entry Permit, etc. ready to proceed by military train and ship via Dover, Calais to Bad Oeynhausen, Headquarters of the British Army of the Rhine; final destination Lubbecke.

Our party, an assorted collection of about a dozen women, was escorted to Dover by a young army lieutenant who throughout the journey did his level best to ignore our presence. On arrival he lined us up on the quay and barked: "Wait here!"

"What you got there, Sir?" shouted a beefy sergeant striding along.

"Nothing much only twelve WOs" replied the lieutenant, surveying his squad with the utmost contempt.

I looked around in shocked amazement. Every man jack a warrant officer! and I had thought that I'd been exceptionally privileged to start my new career at so exalted a rank in the pecking order.

"I have a horrid feeling we are the lowest form of life in the CCG," said the plump round-faced girl standing in line next to me, who'd already lost one of the brass buttons off her too tight jacket. She was right. It had become cruelly apparent that in the eyes of the army we represented the nasty scrapings from the bottom of the barrel, and merited no better treatment.

She told me her name was Mary Atkins, she came from Manchester, and was going to be a typist in something called PRISC. "I don't know what it means," she added.

"I'm a Billet Supervisor Grade 4 in something called LAU, whatever that means! What made you join the CCG, Mary?"

"Well, really just for the adventure and excitement. My father didn't want me to join; he was in the army during the war and was taken prisoner. He hates the Germans. He still calls them Huns, and Krauts . . . . that's what they called the guards in the camp. Dad thought I might be attacked, or something in Germany."

"Are you scared?" I asked her.

"Not really, but I just don't know what to expect."

"I don't think any of us do," I said. "Did your mother mind your joining?"

"She was very upset but she didn't try to stop me. She and my father had a row about it, they're always having rows, so I really wanted to leave home. After all, I am twenty-two."

R. L. Stevenson thought it better to travel hopefully than to arrive, which probably made sense if he was on one of his travels with a donkey in Spain, not on a military train. From Calais we travelled across Northern France, Belgium and Holland, sitting up all night, crammed six aside in the carriage. At each frontier armed police and guards boarded the train holding us up for long tedious periods while they checked our papers in a frenzy of rubber stamping.

The train was what the Germans call a Bummel Zug — a casual strolling train, and stroll it did, on and on into Germany through North Rhine, Westphalia and the big industrial cities of the Ruhr, Aachen, Krefeld, Duisberg, Essen, Dortmund —

all had suffered relentless bombing.

At Duisberg we were sitting in the Naafi restaurant car enjoying our first taste and look of creamy white bread with unrationed butter, when the train slowly drew to a halt. Immediately a hard object like a bullet smacked against the window, rudely shattering our complacency. On the platform wedged closely together stood a great crowd of people. With their identical pallid faces and shabby dark clothes, individual lines were blurred into a solid greyish mass. They stared at us with scowling expressions and one or two shook their fists.

"That was a stone. Pull the blinds down," ordered an officer. "There may be more."

"But why?" enquired Mary innocently.

"Because they're hungry and seeing you lot stuffing yourselves drives them mad."

"Oh poor things, how terrible!" exclaimed Mary. Then as the train began to move she suddenly stood up and pulling down the window began to toss slices of bread onto the platform as if feeding gulls at the seaside, and like bickering gulls the people fought one another to catch the bread in mid-air, a harrowing sight which had the impact of a scene from a television film designed to shock the armchair viewer out of his apathy.

Mary was reprimanded and told not to do such a stupid thing again. As we passed through more stations we saw always the same sullen faces on the platforms, staring at us as though mesmerized by invaders from another planet. Were they hoping to catch a train to somewhere, or had they come out of curiosity to gaze at yet another batch of victors arriving to take charge of their country?

Later we were to witness the extraordinary sight of hundreds of people, men women and children, fighting their way onto already full trains, scrambling onto the buffers, even competing for a place on top of the coaches as they set off for the country in search of food. I wandered how many would fall off, and what would happen to those on the roof when the train went through a tunnel.

At Bad Oeynhausen, in Westphalia, our party was met by a CCG uniformed girl who, after introducing herself as Eileen, a welfare officer, proceeded to tick our names off a list. When she came to mine she said she would be taking me to my billet in Lubbecke, but first would I mind if we drove about twenty kilometers into the country to a farm where Carl, her driver, had told her the farmer had a puppy for sale.

I am not quite sure what I had expected to find on first setting foot in defeated Germany — arrogant hostile faces certainly, angry mobs and even perhaps to be attacked or shot at. In the British press there had been lurid stories about 'werewolves', guerilla fighters who had gone into hiding with the object of carrying on the fight. But surely not the fortune-teller gazing into her crystal ball could have discerned even a cloudy image of my being taken straight away to see a man about a dog!

"You'd better have your suitcase with you on the seat," Eileen said. "There's not much room for luggage. These Volkswagens have the engine in the boot."

The little 'beetles' were almost the only cars on the roads. With few exceptions, such as doctors and others considered to have priority, there were no cars for the Germans. The 'people's cars' had been commandeered as runabouts for the use of the allies. Hitler's promise of a car for every worker had gone the way of all his other promises.

As we drove through the peaceful countryside we could see no sign of war devastation. The fields, cultivated in narrow parallel strips, stretched to the horizon, with here and there an isolated timbered barn. Although conversation with Carl was limited, for he didn't seem to understand much English, Eileen appeared to be on quite intimate terms with him, which I found surprising. At regular intervals she lit a cigarette which she carefully placed in his mouth. I had imagined most Germans to be blond, but he was a small dark-haired young man with a sallow complexion. I noticed that his thin jacket was badly frayed at the elbows and cuffs. He looked very poor and unhealthy.

On arrival at the farmhouse we were met by the farmer who exactly matched my image of a prosperous German country-man. He was the only healthy-looking person I'd seen so far. He wore a green felt hat with the familiar 'shaving brush' stuck in the back and a green loden cloth jacket with knee breeches and stockings. At his heels, yapping excitedly, trotted a little brown dachshund. "Rühe, Fritzi!" he kept shouting to the puppy. "Rühe." The ensuing dialogue sounded like fractured German, even to my ignorant ears. The only words I understood were 'coffee', 'cigarettes', which the farmer kept repeating. The haggling went on for some time until eventually Eileen said "Auf Wiedersehen" and we returned to the car without the puppy.

"I offered him two hundred marks for it," Eileen said. "That's what I got for selling a bottle of gin on the black market, but he wouldn't take it. He said it was no use, he wanted a pound of coffee and a couple of packets of cigarettes. I should have known better."

"Why didn't he want the money?"

"Oh because the German Reichmarks are pretty well worthless. You see there's absolutely nothing of value to buy with them except souvenirs, wood carvings and other ornaments. It's only people like us who want that sort of thing. In any case the farmers are the only people who have plenty of food. They're all right. All they want is coffee, tea, and cigarettes."

"Then where is all the food?"

"On the farms. You see the farmers are holding it back because they know the allies are pledged to introduce a currency reform in order that money will really be worth something. In the same way the manufacturers are holding back goods. That's why there's almost nothing in the shops. The allies are waiting for the Russians to agree, but they are taking their time."

Eileen seemed very knowledgeable about the state of affairs in West Germany. She went on talking, but all the useful information swept over my weary head. I yearned only to reach the old city of Lübeck, smell the Baltic Sea and then sleep till the next day.

"Lübeck!" she laughed. "What gave you that idea? We are going to Lubbecke in Westphalia."

My mistake, but it no longer mattered. I was beginning to feel that to arrive anywhere would be an achievement. The billet was a solid square house in the country outside the town of Lubbecke. Once the home of a wealthy Nazi, it had been requisitioned by the British Military Government as a sort of half-way house for CCG recruits waiting to take up their posts.

The most memorable event during the two idle weeks spent there was my first and only bath. Jaded and travel-stained after that awful train journey, I had been contemplating the pleasure of a long hot soak. The huge bathroom had a white marble floor and cream tiled walls. Over the black, sunken bath, spacious enough to accommodate a team of rugby players, hung a weird set of chromium fitments like chandeliers, which I took to be showers. The taps disguised as dolphins' heads gleamed like polished silver — maybe they were. It was a bathroom straight out of those old extravagant Hollywood films which usually included a scene of the star reclining in a sunken bath, her nakedness discreetly enveloped in bubbles of foam.

With this alluring picture in mind, I turned on the hot tap — at least it was marked ''Heiss''. Not a drop of water emerged from the dolphin's mouth. I tried the cold tap — ''Kalt'' — nothing. Oh well, perhaps the showers would work; no good, their various knobs and taps seemed to be stuck fast. While despondently putting on my dressing-gown, there was a knock on the door. Outside stood a bent old man carrying in each hand a chipped enamelled bucket from which rose clouds of steam. With a mighty effort he heaved the water into the bath where it lay in the black vastness almost invisible to the naked eye, barely adequate to encompass one naked toe.

About ten of us were billeted in that grand house and we had absolutely nothing to do except eat our unpalatable rations, and go for long country walks in twos and threes for 'safety'. In this lotus-eating paradise, 'work' manifestly belonged to that class of words regarded as unmentionable. Deciding the time had come to mention it, I approached Eileen. She registered incomprehension and said disapprovingly, ''It's early days yet, you know.''

At the end of the second week, however, she informed me that the following Monday a car would be coming to take me to Bünde, the small town where I was to start my job as a Billet Supervisor (Grade 4). I hadn't yet discovered any higher, or lower grades!

I was the only passenger in the Volkswagen, and sat in the back behind the young German driver.

''Krieg nicht gut'' he muttered from time to time. I

understood that much. Krieg as 'Blitzkrieg' had become part of war-time English.

"Nein," I replied, "war isn't good." It seemed the only thing to say.

"Alles kaput" he went on in a melancholy tone, repeating it over and over again with loud sighs, "Everything destroyed."

Nothing had happened to make me feel uneasy, but travelling along those lonely country roads, I began to wonder about the young driver. What was his background? Had he been a Nazi? Did he still feel hatred towards the British? I felt my imagination running out of control. At any moment he could stop the car, drag me into a wood and kill me, at the very least! What I didn't know was that all the drivers for military government had been thoroughly vetted. Many of them were refugees who would certainly do nothing to jeopardise their jobs. Anyway, we arrived safely in Bünde, where he delivered me to my billet, situated in a compound surrounded by a high barbed-wire fence.

Bünde — 'Bundy' to the troops — a pleasant little country town, had been seemingly completely taken over by the British. CCG and army uniforms were everywhere. Hilda, the local welfare officer, had been with the CCG in Germany almost since the end of the war. With her tall slim figure and masses of reddish gold hair she was a very striking person, unmistakably English. Her open and direct manner radiated confidence. You felt there was absolutely nothing she couldn't cope with. Instead of the horrible CCG uniform she was wearing a smart khaki battledress top with a narrow skirt, which made me feel even more awkward and clownish than usual.

Hilda told me that before the war she had been a welfare officer in a big factory near London. She briefed me on my job.

"A lot of the houses in Bünde have been requisitioned for CCG personnel. You'll be looking after the billets of Public Safety Branch. Some of the men in these are ex-policemen, and their function is to help to control and reorganise the German police and security forces. You'll have to inspect the houses regularly and try to make them as comfortable as possible. A good many ordinary domestic fittings are in short supply, or don't work. You'll probably have to do quite a bit of scrounging; also supervise the cleaning by the German girls.

You'll get the cleaning materials etc. from the quartermaster's stores. Just write a chit to the sergeant for what you need; but before you get anything new you'll have to take back the worn out things such as brooms, mops, floor-cloths. Some of the houses haven't any curtains, but in the stores they have rolls of green and white striped material which was used for some war-time purpose. Just do the best you can. Come to me if you have any problems.'' Seeing that I didn't appear to be brimming over with enthusiasm, she asked, ''What sort of job have you had?''

''Well, I'm a trained teacher. I've been in broadcasting, and during the war I worked as a personnel officer in a large aircraft factory.''

''Oh no,'' Hilda laughed, ''not another one!''

''What do you mean, not another one?''

''Another square peg in a round hole. The CCG, is full of them. I was talking to a chap the other day who told me he just couldn't cope with his job. He was something in the education branch, which is supposed to be re-educating the Germans. 'I don't know nowt about edication,' he said, 'I'm a master builder!' Now the poor chap's drowning his sorrows in drink. Sometimes I think that in London they matched people with jobs by drawing names out of a hat. Quite a few of the chaps in Public Safety Branch are from the North. They always refer to it as 'Pooblic Seftey', and that's what everyone calls it now! There are some shady characters among them who are just out for what they can get.''

''Well, this master builder had better change places with me. I want to get into education.''

''Why on earth did you take this job?''

''Well, that's all they had to offer me. I just saw this one old man and he didn't seem to know much about anything. He told me they had lost all my papers.''

''You don't say!'' Hilda laughed. ''Where have I heard that before!''

''The recruiting in London seems to have been an awful muddle. How soon do you think I can get another job?''

''You haven't even started this one yet! Once you're in a slot I can tell you it's extremely difficult to get out of it and into another one. I can't think why you're not officer status.''

"I seem to be a whole lot of things. I'm a warrant officer, a Billet Supervisor and in LAU, Grade 4. I don't even know what it means!

"Oh, that's just Local Administration Unit, don't forget we're all civil servants. This is a bureaucratic set-up."

"I've discovered that already" I said, "but I just haven't come out to Germany to be a sort of housekeeper/nanny to British personnel. I mean, it does seem a ridiculous anti-climax."

Hilda said that she understood and would try to help by introducing me to the 'right people' but added it might take months before anything happened, leaving me with that well-known sinking feeling.

The CCG appeared to be run by hordes of young girls, mostly employed as secretaries, typists and clerks in numerous administration offices. No doubt they were necessary in large numbers because the administration of Germany at that time was the chief business of the allies. Every facet of German life, at any rate, in the British zone, was controlled and in the process of being reorganised. This was done by sub-dividing the various major divisions of the CCG into branches or departments, each dealing with one particular aspect of organised life: Education, Broadcasting, the Press and Information, Theatre, Transport, Cinema, Police, Monuments and Fine Arts and so on, the last named concerned with trying to retrieve valuable works of art which had unaccountably vanished; and, the sorting of 'good' monuments from those in disgrace. One branch entitled Public Utilities was usually referred to as Public Futilities!

Another branch could occasionally produce the odd slightly bizarre spectacle — a rotund bosomy lady — the badge on her uniform sleeve boldly proclaiming 'Manpower'! A department whose function was to deal with women's special interests, had the somewhat ambiguous title — Women's Affairs.

One of the CCG's numerous scandals erupted in the mysteriously named Disposals Branch. It was alleged that various items not listed for disposal had in fact been disposed of, and — profitably!

The general educational standard of many CCG people

struck me as being pretty low. On arrival they were not unnaturally confused. They showed little interest in the Germans, and had no idea how to behave towards them. In the billets, German women and girls were employed as maids, cooks, cleaners etc. They were often of a more superior type and better educated than our girls. They were doing these jobs because there was no other work available, and at least they got food and other perks.

The British girls were inclined to treat them in a high-handed manner, which in their ignorance they imagined was the correct way to deal with servants.

The job turned out to be as futile and boring as I had feared, but in no way could it be described as hard work. Every morning at about ten o'clock I started my round of inspection.

"Oh come on in, my dear, I'm just having a drink. What would you like?" was the stock greeting from Pooblic Seftey. All ranks in the CCG received a generous weekly drinks ration, spirits, tax and duty free, at around six shillings a bottle. You could flog the stuff on the black market, barter it, or drink it. Most people drank it. After my morning's 'work', I would usually arrive back at the billet a little unsteady on the feet, and had to lie down before lunch to recharge my batteries in time for the afternoon's repeat performance.

Electric light bulbs, washing-up bowls, brushes, floor-cloths, and curtains were the things most needed. I couldn't get a replacement even for a smelly ragged floor-cloth without taking it along to the quartermaster's stores and writing out a chit which had to be signed by the sergeant, a retiring elusive fellow, rarely to be seen on the premises. Possibly he was enjoying a taste of *la dolce vita* in a Schloss deep in the forest, occupying his time with deer-hunting and shooting.

There was an army style inventory for each billet, graded according to the rank of the occupants. While waiting for the sergeant to return from his day's sport, I casually picked up one of the lists from the usual pile of 'bumf', thinking I might have missed some special comforts for my billets, and read . . . . .
BOWLS
    Washing 1
    Pudding 2

BRUSHES
>   Floor 2
>   Lavatory 1
>   Dust 1

Boats caused a thrill of anticipation. Which lucky ranks would be issued with a boat? But alas . . . . .

BOATS
>   Gravy 1
>   Sauce 2

Further down POTS produced some nice juxtapositions . . .

POTS
>   Cooking 3
>   Chamber 2
>   Flower 1

One rough diamond had asked me to fix up some curtains in his bedroom, complaining that the German girls in the house opposite were in the habit of staring at him as he was getting undressed, a likely story. They couldn't be that depraved — not in 'Bundy'!

Luxuries such as ready-made curtains were, of course, unobtainable but I managed to get hold of a roll of the thin green and white material which Hilda had mentioned. I was not looking forward to making them by hand, something I'd never attempted. Only a few of the personal effects belonging to the families who had inhabited these houses were to be found now. Anything they hadn't managed to take with them had probably been looted. However, while exploring a cellar I came across an ancient treadle-machine which appeared to be in reasonable working order. Although I had never operated one, I managed to run up a couple of curtains and proudly took them along to the billet. The man thanked me, saying he would put them up himself.

A few days later, walking past the house, I glanced up — no curtains. Annoyed I went in, demanding to know why he hadn't yet put them up.

"Oh those," he said. "They were much too good for the likes of me. I gave them to the girl-friend. She's going to make herself a dress out of them for the dance on Saturday.''

As the curtains disappeared from the windows, so the smart green and white striped dresses in the streets of Bünde multiplied. Almost the only other material to be obtained was surplus parachute silk in the muted brown and green splodges of the usual camouflage design, which the women used to make into bras and pants. It was touching to be given a set by one of the cleaners.

The time spent exploring the countryside was the most enjoyable part of my stay in Bünde. Hilda had an official Volkswagen for her own special use, and at weekends, taking a picnic lunch, we would go for long drives. Travelling along the empty country roads, often lined with apple trees, we rarely met another car — a reminder of that long-forgotten pastime — motoring pleasure.

One day we visited the site of the famous Möhne Dam which had been a major target for the RAF bomber squadron, the 'Dambusters', led by Wing Commander Guy Gibson. It was astounding to see the massive concrete structure neatly split as if by a gigantic axe. When the pent-up water was released, a vast area of land became flooded. Guy Gibson, who returned safely was decorated. From a subsequent raid he did not return.

We were fortunate to have plenty of leave, and as during the war years we had been deprived of foreign travel, most of us seized the opportunity to spend our leave in neighbouring countries; Belgium, Holland and Denmark in particular. Hilda and I decided to go to Rome, travelling all the way by train. After spending a night in Milan we caught the 'Italian Rapido'. During the long journey, we quickly picked up a few words of Italian, the key ones being literally, *Occupato* and *Libero*. It was an uncomfortable trip in the shaking, overcrowded train, with the WC *Occupato* all the way to Rome! As soon as people realised we were English they tried to start up a conversation, which because of obvious language difficulties, never got very far. The most quoted word was Churchill. People would just say 'Churchill . . . great man . . . . good man' and then raise their fingers in the familiar V sign, which struck us as rather odd in view of the fact that their country had been fighting on the other side.

After a few days spent sightseeing, we began to feel that we were becoming satiated with 'Culture', and decided to take a whole day off to go to Anzio, the nearest seaside town. But the next morning we were in for a surprise. Had another war started, or were they making a film? It could have been either.

The streets were seething with mobs of people waving flags and shouting unintelligible slogans. Tanks, armoured cars and gun-carriers thundered past the hotel windows. Adding colour to the grim scene were the vivid reds of flags, caps and shirts.

"What's going on?" we asked the manager who was cowering behind his desk probably seeing himself as number one for the firing squad.

"It is the communists — a demonstration to welcome their leader, Togliati."

"Looks more like a war," Hilda said. "Anyway, I don't care about Tog . . . whatever his name is. We'll go before things get rough."

"But, Madame, you must not leave the hotel today. It will be dangerous. There could be shooting. The army is there."

"Oh nonsense!" replied Hilda in her usual breezy manner. "We'll take a taxi." She made it sound as if we were just off for a day's shopping at Harrods.

"There will be no taxis today, Madame. They will be afraid to go on the streets. They could not even get on the streets. You can see that."

"All right, we'll walk to the station. Charge!" Hilda commanded, and meekly I followed my leader through the swing doors into battle. "Adios!" she flung at the manager.

The wretched man threw up his hands in a gesture of hopelessness clearly implying that what he'd aways heard he had now discovered for himself: the British were indeed crazy.

It was not easy to make headway through the dense crowds but Hilda, pushing both arms forward and round in a sort of breast-stroke and repeating in an authorative tone, *"Permesso, Permesso,"* cleaved a path like a swimmer in a rough sea. So impressed were the Romans at the spectacle of these formidable

Anglo-Saxon females that they fell back to let us through. In this manner we made our way to the station, Hilda alternating between *"Permesso"* and murmuring graciously with a bow to the respectful crowds, *"Gracia, Gracia."*

Miraculously a train stood ready and willing to depart for Anzio.

After days filled to the brim with sightseeing, it was refreshing to swim in the sea and lie stretched out in the sun. Hilda remained her usual imperturbable self, but a single question kept pestering me. 'What would we find on our return to Rome?' A scenario was shaping up in my mind, Hilda and I as extras or 'bit' players dodging bullets, hiding in dark passageways, flinging ourselves flat on the ground, eventually to be marched off, hands up, to wait in some fearful dungeon for the British Consul to come to our rescue. Hilda of course wasn't in the least bothered.

"I bet it'll all be over," she said. "These continentals don't know how to control their emotions. They've never even heard of the stiff upper lip."

Hilda was entitled to feel smug about her prediction.

In the eternal city, all appeared to be sweetness and light — almost. The war-like scene that we had left behind had faded into one of peaceful dissipation. The tanks were parked, the drivers presumably having gone off to join their comrades in slaking their thirst. At the pavement cafés, empty bottles rolled about on the tables, and in the streets small boys were playing football with them. Exhausted and drunken men sprawled over chairs, their mouths hanging open. Red caps and flags lay crumpled in the dust. A good time had clearly been had by all.

"What did I tell you?" Hilda said. "They're just small boys playing war-games," and Hilda, I reflected, was one of the last surviving members of that endangered species — the English governess!

We returned to Bünde tired and dishevelled. It had been a tedious journey and trains in those early days of peace lacked most of the normal amenities. Bed was uppermost in my mind, just to stretch out for hours and hours but, judging by the sounds emanating from my bedroom, it seemed to be a long way from some other people's thoughts. Opening the door I plunged into a swinging party.

"Hello, didn't expect you back till tomorrow," someone shouted. "Hope you don't mind, but we moved into your room because it is the biggest. We couldn't keep all these gatecrashers out."

Even surrounded by that din, I could have lain down on my bed, and at once fallen into what I was beginning to hope would be an everlasting sleep, but there was no bed in its usual place; it had been stood up against a wall. A man thrust a glass into my hand, spilling half the drink on the floor. Well, there was only one thing to do, admit defeat — if you couldn't beat 'em, join 'em.

For some time sinister rumours had been circulating around Bünde that 'married families' were shortly coming out. Why 'married families'? Were 'unmarried families' to be excluded? All it meant was that the wives and children of men serving in the CCG were going to be allowed to set up house in Germany, so that family life could be resumed; but far from this news bringing universal satisfaction it was greeted in some quarters with consternation. Long-standing liaisons and friendships with German girls had to be sorted out, involving a good deal of adjustment and hasty reorganisation.

More and more houses were requisitioned. Bill, a male supervisor, and I were presented with a skeleton key supposed to be capable of opening any lock, however obdurate. It was a simple looking gadget, a small metal rod hooked at one end. We had to inspect the houses; see that they were properly cleaned by the German women; supervise the arrival of Naafi furniture, if required; and generally make the houses as habitable as possible.

"I don't know how to use this thing," I told Bill, after several abortive attempts to open firmly closed doors. "I'm not in the habit of breaking open locks."

"It's easy," Bill said, as with no fuss at all, he inserted the key and flung open the door. "There you are!"

"How did you do that, Bill?"

"Oh, just practice."

Hardly daring to ask, I said, "What did you do before the war?"

"I was an all-in wrestler."

"What!"

"Yes, that is until I joined up. I used to do a bit of wrestling in the army too."

"What made you come out here?"

"Oh, I heard the pickings were good — easy Frauleins, plenty of cheap booze. I like women, but not British ones — too stuffy, can't let their hair down. These German girls will sell body and soul for a bar of Cadburys, or a packet of fags — decent girls too, well brought up."

"Well," I said, "the situation is rather different here," but he wasn't listening. He'd disappeared into another room.

"Hey, come and look here!" he called. "I wonder this hasn't been nicked." He was staring down at an intricately patterned wall-to-wall carpet. "I reckon that's genuine Persian," he said, running his hand over the thick pile, "or could be Indian." Then taking out a large pocket-knife, he began to slide it under the carpet close to the wall.

"What are you doing?"

"I'm going to take this carpet up."

"But you can't do that!"

"Why not? I want it for my collection. I've already got quite a few. Next time I go on leave I'm going to take them back with me."

"But someone will find out."

"Who? I'll tell the sergeant that we need a Naafi carpet here because the old one's gone. You can't bring an English family in to a house without a carpet, can you? I had a letter from my wife today and she wants to come out here with our daughter but I'm going to put her off. It would be awkward with Helga." When he'd got the carpet rolled up he stowed it away in a corner saying he would come back to fetch it.

"What about the family who used to live here? They may come home one day. Everything else has gone. You might at least leave them their carpet."

"Why should I? The bastards! I saw what they did to Coventry, my home town."

"I seem to remember that we bombed a few German cities," I said, "Dresden, Hamburg, Berlin and all those towns in the Rühr."

"Well, the Jerries asked for it. They started the whole business. Now, let's see what else there is." He stumped upstairs and after a few minutes was down again. "Nothing there,'' he announced. ''This was all I found.'' It was a small photo frame. As he brushed the dust off the cracked glass with his sleeve a faded yellowish picture came to light. ''That must be the whole family,'' he said. ''Father in the Luftwaffe uniform. God, he probably took part in the raids on Coventry.''

''The wife looks attractive,'' I said, studying the group. ''And the children are gorgeous. I wonder where they are now.''

''Who cares?'' he said, hurling the photograph at the wall. ''Let's go back to my billet and have a drink.''

Bill's attitude was not unusual. I was mixing with many people like him. The words rehabilitation, re-education, democratisation, meant nothing to them. In their view the Germans were the cause of all the trouble and misery, and now they'd been defeated and their country occupied. That was as it should be. We, they argued, had suffered and worked hard to win the war so why shouldn't we enjoy ourselves? All very understandable but, nevertheless, it seemed a pity because, as far as one could judge by the people one met and the general atmosphere of Anglo-German relations, most of the Germans appeared to be ready to respect us. They were doing their best to adapt to, what must have been for them a humiliating situation, and they were willing to co-operate in the remaking of their lives; but they needed all the help they could get.

The official policy formulated by the allies as early as September 1944, was non-fraternization with the German population. Although I'd heard of it I'd never given it a thought in my relationships with young Germans. However, enlightenment came while supervising the clearing up after an officers' party. I noticed propped against a glass on the bookcase an official-looking leaflet. It was headed RESTRICTED, and below the impressive title :—
Policy on Relations
between
Allied Occupying Forces
and
Inhabitants of Germany.
(To be distributed to Company Commanders
and their equivalents).

At the foot of the leaflet in small print I read :
This document must not fall into enemy hands.

September 1944

Although well outside the category of company commanders, or even of their equivalents, I felt I had just as much right as they to be informed of the plans made by the high and mighty for this country's future. In London I had been told nothing. A thrill shot through me; I might have been stealing designs for a new secret weapon as furtively I picked up the leaflet and slipped it into my pocket. At least I would take care that it didn't fall into enemy hands!

Living in that small town, as quiet and placid as an English village, it seemed incredible that the military authorities had been concerned for the safety of the occupation forces. They had anticipated resistance with fighting continuing for perhaps a long time, as stated in the leaflet :

Paragraph 3
'The occupying forces must be prepared for civil disorders including sniping and assaults on individuals, sabotage, provoked riots, perhaps even organised raids. Hidden arms will undoubtedly be available.'

Well, all that was news to me! Why did none of it come to pass? Why even directly after the war was resistance negligible? Possibly because the population was weary of conflict and in any case there was a scarcity of fit young men, but more likely the reason could be summed up in one word 'hunger'. Most people, especially those in the cities, had to devote a great deal of their time to foraging for food, often entailing long journeys into the country. In addition they had to fix up somewhere to live and when they had at last found four walls and a roof more or less intact, had literally to paper over the cracks. They had to patch and mend clothes and shoes, make their own soap, grow their own tobacco, and above all, take extra care to see that the children did not suffer.

Paragraph 4 — Non-fraternization
'Definition: Non-fraternization is the avoidance of mingling with Germans upon terms of friendliness, familiarity or intimacy whether individually or in groups. However, it does not demand rough, undignified or aggressive conduct nor the insolent overbearance which has characterized Nazi leadership.'

Paragraph d — Restriction on Contacts
'The following must be prohibited: Visiting German homes, drinking with Germans; shaking hands with them; playing games or sports with them; giving or accepting gifts; attending German dances or other events; accompanying Germans on the street, in theatres, taverns, hotels or elsewhere (except on official business); discussions and arguments with Germans, especially on politics or the future of Germany.'

And to think in my ignorance of all that I had been talking, arguing and actually shaking hands with Germans. It's a wonder I hadn't been court martialled!

How could one avoid shaking hands? It's hard not to take a hand extended to you; almost a reflex action to grasp it. As far as I could see in Germany, everybody shook hands on every possible occasion; workmen did it when arriving at building sites; small boys and girls jumped off bicycles to pump each other's arms; toddlers wobbling into the room to be introduced put out a tentative waving hand; children before going to bed shook hands with their parents; and on birthdays a positive epidemic of handshaking broke out.

Sometimes I was obliged to board one of those fast paternoster lifts — a continuous moving chain of small open-fronted boxes designed to carry two or three people. You had to be quite nippy to get on and off. An absent-minded colleague missed her floor and was carried round and down into the dark bowels of the building before going up again. Hoping to avert being taken for this subterranean ride, I made a habit of getting off at the floor before my destination.

One morning a waiting German acquaintance catching sight

of me ascending rapidly, shot out his hand to grab mine just as my feet reached the level of his head, forcing me into a hairpin bend, half out and half in the contraption.

Warning: Excessive handshaking can damage your health!

Naturally, British soldiers and civilians were busy 'fraternizing' with the local girls. A German girl-friend was known as a 'frat', and mixing with Germans 'fratting'. But then as Kipling said, 'Single men in Barracks don't grow into plaster saints'.

A useful outcome of these relationships was the speed with which the soldiers picked up a good knowledge of colloquial German. On several occasions I happened to be present when a high-ranking officer, faced with a knotty language problem, had unwillingly to summon a corporal or private to act as interpreter for him.

While making my regular house inspections, I sometimes came across quantities of magazines and other literature published by the Nazis before and during the war; most of it blatant propaganda. I used to take a selection home and, with the aid of a dictionary, endeavour to translate at least some of the more sensational-looking headlines.

One photograph in an illustrated magazine showed a party of British army officers with attractive girls seated at a restaurant table, littered with bottles.

The caption read "England's letzte Stunde" — "England's last hour." The article explained that these people were at the Royal Savoy, one of the many London night clubs. It went on "while the military snobs and those in high society amuse themselves in London's West End, the working people huddle in the underground stations to shelter from the bombs of 'our gallant Luftwaffe'."

Another picture showed top-hatted chorus girls pretending to take aim with rifles. The accompanying text informed readers that the girls were illustrating the English popular song "Run, Rabbit, Run" and shooting at the terrible enemy — the Germans.

There was a photograph depicting sixth-form Harrow Schoolboys at roll-call; their straw boaters tilted at varying angles; the boys unfortunately looking particularly weedy and unmanly. Adjacent to this picture was one of young men of the Hitler Youth, stripped to the waist, blond, virile, handsome, marching off to work with shovels over their shoulders. The caption said in effect . . . . . "Look upon this picture and on that. Contrast the effete British boys with our splendid, strong and vigorous Hitler Youth."

Well, effete or virile, British or German was now a matter of indifference. How many of them were dead? Only photographs, but each likeness represented a real life, too young to have borne any responsibility for what had happened. It brought to mind 'The Anthem for Doomed Youth', the moving poem by Wilfred Owen, himself killed in the First World War, 'What passing bell for these who died as cattle?'

Prompted by curiosity I was always on the look-out for mementoes of interest which might throw light on the previous occupants of these solid comfortable houses. Had there been a peremptory knock, on the door and a British officer ordering "Come on, get out"? That was the Nazi way. Some might have been quite young families who were swept helpless into the maelstrom. Others could have been members of the Nazi hierarchy. Who, I wondered, was the head of the house in which I discovered a heavy iron medal about two inches in diameter? It was lying in an open metal box in the cellar. On examining it I saw it had been struck to commemorate the sinking of the *Lusitania*. In relief it showed the liner, her bows lifted out of the water. The inscription below, translated said . . . ."Steamship, *Lusitania,* sunk by German submarine — 5th May 1915", and around the edge of the medal, 'No contraband'. Depicted on the obverse side was a group of top-hatted business men queuing in front of a ticket-office over which were the words 'Cunard Line'. The clerk in the office was a skeleton. "Business over everything" said the caption.

Many years later I read an article in a long established English periodical denying that such a medal had ever been struck by the Germans. It was, claimed the writer, nothing more than a fabrication of British war-time propaganda aimed at inciting hatred towards the Germans for gloating over the deliberate torpedoing of an unarmed civilian liner.

By now I was increasing my efforts to get another job, regularly calling on heads of departments and writing letters to the top brass to complain of my uninteresting work and insisting more out of desperation than conceit, that I considered myself capable of better things. The replies, although expressing sympathy, were generally negative and unhelpful.

Then, as so often happens in the hit and miss business of life, a few casual words coming at the right moment, and the needle of your built-in compass suddenly points in the hoped for direction.

"I've met a Colonel Smith," Hilda remarked, "who's just come back from leave in Holland and he's returning to Hamburg next weekend. He says he can give you a job in the office. It's something called the Broadcasting Control Unit."

"But that's marvellous! Doesn't he want to know more about me?"

"Oh, I told him everything," Hilda went on. "The only trouble will be getting you released from this job and posted to Hamburg in a different branch, but I'll do what I can to speed things up."

Hamburg! It produced the sort of tingling sensation one often gets before the start of a long journey to a strange place, or a new venture of some sort — an amalgam of excitement and elation spiced with apprehension. The process of reconstruction in the city, which 'Hamburgers' like to call the 'Gateway to the World', must be in full swing, and just to play a part, however insignificant, in this immense undertaking was all that I desired. Looking back it could have been a kind of youthful missionary fervour which now rather sadly appears laughable.

More waiting. The weekend came and nothing had happened.

"When do you think my transfer will come through?" I asked Hilda.

"Oh not for ages. It will have to go through the usual channels. It's probably sitting in someone's 'In-tray', or 'Pending'. You see, you'll have to be regraded on a new pay scale and all the rest of it."

"But I can't wait. Colonel Smith might give the job to someone else."

"I shouldn't think so. You'd better hang on. By the way, have you heard about Bill? He was taken off the military train at Bentheim. Something to do with stolen carpets. He may be sent back to UK.''

"Well, that will solve the problem of Helga.''

"Oh, his 'frat'. Yes, poor girl. She'll probably go hungry until she finds someone else.''

I told Hilda that the job had reduced me to a state of frustration and hopelessness, the cleaners complained of being too hungry to work properly and when I did manage to procure things to make the billets more comfortable, basic articles like wash-basins, light bulbs and curtains, they disappeared almost at once, and I had to start all over again.

"I'm grabbing this chance,'' I said, "and going to Hamburg with Colonel Smith. The red tape can catch up with me later.''

"Well, it's highly irregular, but I see your point.''

I was sorry to say goodbye to Hilda; we'd had some good times together and my stay in Bünde had been a peaceful introduction to the country. I hoped we'd meet again, at the same time realising that in the present social upheaval we were all bound to be as ships that pass in the night.

Colonel Smith sat beside his driver in the front of the large Mercedes and I was ordered to sit in the back, which was full of wooden crates containing Dutch gin — his booty from leave in Holland — stacked on the seat and the floor. He didn't bother to enquire whether there was enough space for me, and only by much twisting and turning was I able to squeeze in at all.

Whenever we drove over a bump or pot-hole, which we did frequently, the crates shifted position, the sharp corners jabbing into my ribs and thighs. On this long journey we stopped only once. The colonel and his driver taking a bottle of gin, disappeared into a thick forest. After about twenty minutes they returned in high spirits singing a tune which vaguely resembled 'Deutschland uber Alles'. The spirit in the bottle had sunk considerably. Catching sight of an old boy by the roadside gawping at them, they raised their arms in the Nazi salute. He stood and stared open-mouthed before shambling off, no doubt to tell his mates of this extraordinary happening — British soldiers had given him the Nazi salute!

For distraction from that uncomfortable ride I turned my thoughts to Hamburg. What would it be like? How would the job turn out? I knew nothing about the city except that it had been a significant target for the RAF — the terrible thousand-bomber raids. The reorganization of broadcasting would be vitally important. Under the Nazis it had been controlled and dominated by propaganda. If I could manage to get a foot in the door of the radio station it would surely lead to something interesting with scope for initiative.

The next pot-hole, more like a bomb-crater, put an end to musing; best to relax and adopt the usually sound policy of wait and see.

Part 2

After the rural peace of unspoilt Bünde, the desolation of Hamburg came as a horrifying shock. Having lived and worked in London and Southampton, I was naturally aware of the vast areas of bomb damage in those, and other big cities, but here at first sight it seemed that the whole town had been laid waste, leaving, like Pompeii, only a reminder of what had once been.

We drove along narrow roads flanked by high cliffs of broken brick and masonry. Great steel girders, tangled and twisted like wire wool, had fallen or been blown up into stark surrealist configurations. Many houses were without a front, exposing the rooms on each floor like an old-fashioned doll's house.

Windows, all awry and without glass, stared blankly. There were solitary jagged walls only a few feet high, belonging nowhere and doors leading to nowhere stood open. Church towers, sliced off as if by a sword, were reduced to stumps. Here and there rough black crosses on walls and doors indicated that possibly bodies still lay under the rubble. In places, little shacks with corrugated iron roofs had been thrown together to provide some sort of home. From time to time we caught sight of rats scurrying over the rubble mountains engaged like everyone else, in the endless search for food. The wind whipped up the thick dust of powdered brick and stone, spinning it around in big clouds. People walked, holding handkerchiefs to their mouths. Men and women were shabbily dressed in dark much patched clothes. It was noticeable how many of the men, had an arm or leg missing. Most of the children, although very thin, looked well cared for with neat clean clothes.

Not a German military uniform was to be seen on the streets. The mighty army, navy and air force, no longer existed. Neither was there any sign of the once ubiquitous swastika the hated emblem of the Nazi regime. Fitting perhaps that they should have chosen as their badge of evil a crooked cross.

There *were* houses still standing. The Germans built very solidly. As we neared the Alster, the huge artificial lake in the centre of the city, we could see through the drooping willow trees lining its banks, some tall villa-type houses which, except for blackened walls, appeared to be intact. Surprisingly the yellow brick building of the radio station with its clock tower and aerial seemed undamaged.

"You see that bunker alongside the main building," the colonel said. "That was where the traitor Lord Haw Haw, alias William Joyce, used to broadcast to Britain. 'Germany calling, I have it on good authority that no British bombs will ever fall on Hamburg. Heil Hitler!' " the colonel went on, giving a passable imitation of the smooth oily tones. "Achtung! ....Whoooosh!"

So within these thick concrete walls the man with the greasy voice had sat alone with his microphone night after night broadcasting his absurdly crude propaganda. Ostensibly he never knew that, far from frightening us all his efforts had the opposite effect, being a source of much amusement during those long blacked-out evenings.

"Did you hear Haw Haw last night?" people would ask. "He's sunk the *Ark Royal* again! That's the third time!"

Strangely, through a hole in the bunker roof, soared the trunk of a large tree. They had taken the trouble to build around it, but then, I thought, the Germans must love trees. There was something symbolic in the action of workmen clearing just enough rubble to plant fresh saplings. It's doubtful whether the men thought that way. They were probably inveighing against the authorities and muttering "This is bloody stupid when we could be building a house."

Colonel Smith dropped me at my new quarters. In Hamburg, the CCG personnel lived in army style messes, and the word billet was never heard. My mess was situated in a quiet residential street lined with beautiful chestnut trees, their leaves just starting to turn golden brown, for it was now September.

Outside the small gate leading to the house stood a large black dustbin, and bending over it a distinguished looking man in a dark suit. He could perhaps have been a doctor or professor. He was picking over the contents of the dustbin and putting bits and pieces into his brief-case. I walked past averting my eyes, realising it was a sight one would have to get used to.

I was greeted by the usual supervisor, a rather nondescript woman of about forty with an Irish accent. It was hard to conceal my annoyance, to put it mildly, when she showed me my room containing three other beds. Once you've been a married woman it's not easy to revert to a boarding-school type of life; but I remembered we had been warned that life in Germany would be a communal one, and so it was a case of having to adapt, which to my surprise, I did with comparative ease. The girls were employed as clerks and typists in the various offices of the administration. They chatted ceaselessly of boy-friends, parties and the next leave. However, we all got on well together in a giggly schoolgirl fashion. After dinner, boy-friends would come up to the bedroom and stay till a late hour. With couples drinking and larking around, sleep before midnight, when the men were supposed to go, was impossible. There was no privacy, not even curtains around the beds, an environment unfavourable for love-making. Moreover, the beds offered little encouragement; the mattresses in three sections could have doubled as flagstones. They were commonly known as 'biscuits'. And the job, that was another let-down. It didn't exist. The staff in the office seemed to consist of the colonel and two or three soldiers who drifted in and out in a vague sort of way. Occasionally one of them gave me some letters and papers to file, which I almost certainly put away in the wrong places as there appeared to be a general reluctance to tell me anything, or more likely there was nothing to tell. I couldn't understand why the colonel had brought me here, but said nothing, thinking it best as usual to adopt the wait and see policy. Sometimes he would send me off in his official car on frivolous errands. The car, an immense Maibach, and one of only a few built for top Nazis, was reputed to have belonged to Hermann Goering. Now its lengthy bonnet carried the Union Jack.

Reclining alone in the back I saw myself as a royal personage who should have been acknowledging the cheers of the crowd, raising a hand and gently turning it in that special way adopted by royalty to distinguish it from the more vulgar flapping sort, employed to see Aunt Mary off on the bus; but there were no crowds, only a few expressionless stares.

One afternoon when I had even less to do than usual the thought suddenly came to me, why not write a script? Just a little talk between an English and a German woman — call it perhaps 'From Woman to Woman' — a friendly chat about the small differences in daily life in our respective countries. Now it sounds naive, but in Germany the intimate style of broadcasting had not yet been developed. At least it would demonstrate an effort at understanding. The head of women's programmes offered to translate the script which was given the title 'Von Frau zu Frau'. All went well at the recording session until I came to one of those German words which seem to consist entirely of 'ss' and 'sch' — 'Schlieslich' — when a sea of bubbles welled up into my mouth, resulting in a sound like a stifled sneeze. 'Cut'! shouted the producer, and racked his brains to find a word less bubble-making for an English tongue.

Colonel Smith was clearly impressed with this effort, saying that I should be in 'Education' and that he would speak to the major in charge of the Broadcast and Teaching Aids Department, which had started organising programmes for schools and colleges on the lines of the BBC.

The major agreed to give me a fortnight's trial. So at last I was where I wanted to be — on the creative end of broadcasting. The major's plan was to produce radio plays and features in simple English about daily life in Britain, with all the characters played by British people, thus giving listeners a chance to hear ordinary spoken English. Since the war, it seemed, everyone was keen to know more about Britain and to learn English.

"I don't seem able to get on with this script," he said, puffing on the pipe which was seldom out of his mouth. "See what you can do." It was in at the deep end. Well, I'd asked for it.

The script was to be a documentary about London. I wrote 'Page one', then 'Fade up sound of Big Ben chimes and into traffic noises'.

Striving with words and sound effects to create an impression of London proved exhausting, and took me over a week. In a back-handed compliment the major said it was an improvement on his effort and so, to the rousing tune of 'Old Father Thames', my first radio work was launched on an unsuspecting wavelength.

I worked closely with Franz Reinholz, whom the major had appointed as head of the department, the overall control remaining of course with the British. Every German script had to be vetted to find out whether it contained anything subversive. At times, when the major and his assistant were away from the office, examining films or doing recordings, this task would fall to me. Franz used to bring a script, saying, ''This is urgent. We've got to record it tonight would you please read it and initial it when you've finished?'' As my German didn't yet amount to much more than Ja, Nein, Bitte, Danke, Guten Tag, it was hardly sufficient to enable me to translate many pages devoted to a literary or technical theme. Anyway, I hadn't the vaguest idea of what I was supposed to be looking for, perhaps something like 'Heil Hitler' or 'Deutschland Uber Alles'. After an hour with the dictionary I would have got through half a dozen lines. When Franz returned on the deadline, I hastily initialled the script and wrote OK, much to his amusement. At the same time he used to take the opportunity to collect the cigarette stubs, known as 'Kippens', from the office ashtrays to recycle into his own home-made brand. On the first occasion I took to smoking with a holder he complained that the 'Kippens' were much shorter. He grinned approvingly as I promptly threw the holder into the waste-paper basket.

Although officially I was his controller, we quickly discovered that we operated on the same wavelength, and formed an easy working relationship. He spoke excellent English, 'clothes' being the only word, in spite of all my coaching, that he never managed, pronouncing it 'closes'. Franz always gave the impression that he'd had a relatively comfortable war, at first as a gliding instructor and later in charge of a weather station in a rural area of occupied France, where he was soon accepted by the local people, among whom he made many friends. He liked to tell the story of how, when he was captured by the Americans, they stripped him of all his personal possessions, watch, wallet, papers etc., but left him with his gun! His boyish sense of fun, more English than German, made working together a real pleasure.

At that time because of the shortage of food he was dreadfully thin, and unhappily our mess rations were too meagre to allow for sharing, but some commodities more precious than rubies we in the CCG had in plenty — the solid Naafi fruit-cake and the powerful gin distilled by Messrs Gordon and Booth — perhaps not the ideal diet to build up and sustain an undernourished person; however, never any complaints from Franz and his colleagues.

During our working sessions when things were not going as smoothly as they might, instead of the usual 'coffee', a witches brew of acorns and dried dandelion roots, we would take a 'gin' break.

I confided to Franz that I was having difficulty choosing subjects for the scripts, the writing of which the major had now handed over to me. I thought that young listeners would prefer to hear about people rather than places. He agreed, ''Why don't we have a serial about a typical English family?'' he suggested.

And so the Johnson family was born into the world of make-believe; Mr and Mrs; their daughter Margaret; and son Bob. They did everything an ordinary English family was supposed to do; they drove into the country for picnics, and took holidays at the seaside in boarding houses named 'Seaview' or 'Sunnyside'. On Saturday evenings they went to the pub, the cinema, or had friends in for a drink. Margaret got engaged to the 'wrong man'. Bob bought a motor bike and left home. The happy family broke up.

It was unlucky, that the people chosen from the British community to play these characters were liable at any time to be transferred to another part of the country, resulting every week or so in Mrs Johnson having a brand new husband, or a different brace of children; a state of affairs which brought an avalanche of complaints from listeners clearly disillusioned with this crude representation of English domestic behaviour; one irate lady writing ''If the Johnson family is typical, I am indeed sorry for 'Great' Britain!''

Somewhat discouraged by this adverse reaction, we decided to abandon the family altogether. Not a soul enquired after their fate and no wonder; they were bores. It's so simple to do away with radio characters. There's no mess, no unpleasantness. They can be spirited away like dissidents to Siberia; take a long holiday staying with cousins in New Zealand; or decide to retire to Worthing. If you are really stuck for characters they can even be brought back, having 'changed' in some way to make them more interesting. Should a quick death be needed for somebody particularly nasty you can easily 'shoot' him in the studio. Slamming the piano lid produces a nice clean 'shot'. However, nowadays there are undoubtedly more sophisticated ways of carrying out a studio execution.

Although we had quite a big library of sound effects on tape, it couldn't include all that were needed for every programme, and some had to be improvised 'live' in the studio. When the engineers read the direction in one of my scripts, 'Fade up sound of shipwreck' they nearly went berserk. Another script required the sound of an old mowing-machine, which couldn't be found. The problem was solved by the studio assistant pushing in an ancient machine belonging to her father, and 'mowing' the studio carpet.

I soon learned to be more specific when writing in sound effect directions. The girl operating the tape recording said, "Frau Melrose, you have written here, 'Fade up sound of dog barking'. Is it a little dog or a big dog, an Alsatian, or a terrier-type?" A reasonable query. The same went for babies crying — how old was the baby? Had it got a pain? Simple actions like the pouring out of tea into a cup did not always produce the desired effect. Perhaps the tea-pot would be held too high above the cup, and the resulting gush would be met with loud laughter and rude jokes from the cast.

Still imbued with missionary zeal I felt that the programmes should become more educational. Young people brought up during the Nazi regime would have little knowledge of Britain's social history, and the many contributions made by her citizens to the general welfare. I would do dramatized biographies of famous British people — good people — Elizabeth Fry, more humane prisons; Edward Jenner, discoverer of vaccination against smallpox; Simpson, use of chloroform as an anaesthetic; Florence Nightingale, her work for nurses and wounded soldiers; and I would throw in a few heroines, Grace Darling and Edith Cavell. I put the idea to Franz, "Yes, it's all right, but I don't like the title," he said.

"What, you mean 'Famous British People'?''

"No, young people are becoming more cynical. They would think it propaganda," and so I changed the title of the series to 'Famous People'. Funny they should all turn out to be British!

For the younger children I invented two characters who week after week, would remain unchanged. I called them Henry and Barbara, because I'd discovered these names were the same in German and I thought it would make the English characters seem less foreign to the children.

There was never a dull moment in their lives. Henry especially, was always deciding to 'take up things'; keeping chickens; painting his own pictures; doing woodwork; making pots; but nothing ever went right; the chickens escaped and laid their eggs under hedges; his paintings were misunderstood by the neighbours; his beautiful glowing sunset, mistaken for a fried egg; the legs of his tables were seldom of equal length, causing visitors' coffee cups to go into a gentle slide overboard; and nobody, not even Barbara, could find a use for his pots.

Henry always spoke directly to the children like a friend, and it was gratifying how quickly his popularity spread. The children wrote letters to him in their best school English, often illustrated with funny little drawings, and they were curious to know more about him.

"Dear Henry," wrote a boy called Gunther. *"We wish to know have you a woman and children?"* An understandable little *faux pas,* considering that in German 'woman' and 'wife' are embodied in the one word — 'Frau'.

Others wrote requesting a photograph, or giving him advice. I used to play a little game, replying to the letters on official Hamburg Radio paper, headed imposingly Norddeutscher Rundfunk, Abteilung Schulfunk' and signing, 'With love from Henry'.

We found that many adults were also keen listeners, earnestly trying to improve their English. Sometimes while travelling around or waiting for a tram I would catch the names Henry and Barbara and prick up my ears. It was frustrating not to be able to follow the dialogue, but judging from the speakers' expressions they usually seemed amused.

Before long we received a number of letters mostly from teachers enquiring whether Henry and Barbara were married, or were they father and daughter, or brother and sister, or even uncle and niece? Strangely enough, up till then their relationship had never entered my head, but now something had to be done about it; they had just been away together. Franz had no doubts. In order to uphold the strict moral standards expected of the British they should enter the state of holy matrimony forthwith!

Queries about Henry's job also arose. What kind of work did he do? It was never mentioned in the plays, hardly surprising for I had made another serious omission. I had not given him a job. He was so busy with other things, I don't think he would have had the time for one.

In the meantime Henry and Barbara's success story had even reached the British Press — at least the *Daily Mail,* which printed a short column with the headline, 'Typically British!' referring to Henry's perpetual state of unemployment and implying that such a character with his apparent reluctance to work would do little for the reputation of the British male abroad!

The major asked if I would like to attend one of the courses in Brunswick designed to instruct the Occupation Forces in the history and social structure of Germany, and generally explore the 'German problem'. I jumped at the idea; it would be a chance to see another part of the country and to meet people in the many different branches of the CCG.

Originally a training centre for Hitler Youth Leaders, the college was a stark modern building with every amenity; big hall and stage; electric organ; cinema; lecture rooms; heated indoor swimming-pool.

On the first day we assembled to hear a talk from the commandant. Among the 'students' was a good sprinkling of grey and white heads, and a glance at the lists on the board showed that many held high ranks in the services.

We were divided into syndicates, about ten in each, and given a specific subject to discuss on which we had to formulate an opinion and summarise it in a document to be produced at the end of the week, when all syndicates would have the opportunity of tearing each other's wordy promulgations to pieces in a general discussion. Our syndicate had as a subject to examine, the new German Basic Law which contained a hundred and forty-six articles, each made up of several paragraphs. At our first sitting we got through four. However, in our free time, assisted by an unlimited supply of strong drink to lubricate the windmills of the mind, it was extraordinary how many vital points we uncovered which had apparently been completely overlooked by the Allied High Command.

Over toast and marmalade a hitherto reticent student would suddenly come out with :

"You know, I think paragraph (a) brackets, article 56, page 11, of the Occupation Statute contains a dangerous loophole," at once triggering off an excited argument.

In the second week there appeared on the timetable the ominous headline 'Student Lectures'.

We were assured that these would be purely voluntary talks to be given by students about their work, but the method of getting volunteers turned out to be not unlike that in the army: the sergeant, pointing a finger at his victims, bawls, "I want three volunteers for this job, you and you and you."

When it was discovered that I worked in broadcasting, I became one of those unfortunates picked on to give a lecture. Following the mostly earnest high-powered dissertations of the brass hats, the exploits of Henry and Barbara 'had 'em rolling in the aisles'. All this intellectual activity was interspersed with the usual cocktail parties, dances and so on; winding up with a dinner to say farewell to Mr Robert Birley, formerly Head of Eton, and educational adviser to the CCG.

I found the course well worthwhile and thoroughly enjoyable. I think it left most of us with a deeper understanding of the so-called 'German problem'.

One question had not been answered, and perhaps never will be: 'How it was that such a highly intelligent and civilised people, from whose ranks have come many of the world's most brilliant musicians, artists, writers and philosophers, could have backed so overwhelmingly a fanatical dictator with the monstrous intent to annihilate the whole Jewish race?' — 'The Final Solution.'

A malicious trick of fate to decree an exceptionally harsh winter for 1947, piling on the agony while resistance was still at a low ebb. Icy winds from Russia swept over the North German Plain. The Alster lake and the canals intersecting the city froze.

For a time even the Rhine was frozen, making it impossible for the barges to bring the coal from the Ruhr.

During this bitter winter the daily struggle to get enough to eat intensified. When the wind wasn't too strong the frozen lake would be dotted with chairs on which crouched muffled figures, dangling fishing-lines through hacked out holes in the ice. I never saw a catch. Maybe all the fish were frozen.

For weeks there was little heating or lighting in the city. Our mess had none.

The discomfort of being permanently chilled to the bone was increased by a common affliction which became known as "Hamburg throat', caused by the wind whirling around the dust from the vast acreage of rubble. As with desert dust, there was no escape; it permeated everything.

In the offices we sat huddled in overcoats. At last I was grateful for that despised uniform, but even with the temperature several degrees below zero I could never bring myself to wear the sloppy beret with its cheap metal badge. The Germans, their heads covered with an assortment of fur hats and caps, some with ear-flaps, Russian style, would often stop in amazement pointing to my bare head and muttering no doubt the German equivalent of nut-case! The ladies, for the most part, seemed to favour headgear resembling inverted chamber pots, and mannish felt trilbys worn clamped down over the ears. Fur coats were clearly home-made from a miscellany of tatty skins stitched together patchwork fashion — a poor old tabby cat, perhaps in the company of a fox, a couple of grey squirrels, and a family of brown bunnies.

Shoes presented the biggest clothing difficulty, impossible to buy and difficult to make. People were obsessed with them and would often stare down at your shoes before looking at your face. The wearing of trousers would have been prevented a lot of distress from the cold, but it was not yet the fashion for women, and didn't appear to have occurred to anyone.

During those freezing weeks without heating most of us in the mess went to bed directly after dinner, usually accompanied by a bottle of gin or whiskey and a pack of cards. There was something pleasantly decadent about lolling on beds wrapped in blankets, drinking and smoking over a game of Vingt-et-un in the flickering light of half a candle — the ration for the evening. With the arrival of boy-friends a minor orgy would develop, and continue far into the night.

For the Germans, suffering from a shortage of food and everything else, the intense cold was the last straw, but as usual the struggle for survival had to go on. The luckiest were those in accommodation, possessing one of the traditional tiled wood-burning stoves. Fuel was not hard to find, sticks and logs from the countryside, broken up doors and window-frames off the rubble heaps — the stove would consume the lot, giving back an even warmth. In fact, I spent many cosy evenings with German friends in such rooms, being warmer there than in the mess. Coal was so scarce that when a consignment did arrive the news spread by jungle drum from house to house. People would trail the lorry, hoping for lumps to fall off. In the street outside the mess I once observed a driver deliberately take his lorry over a small pile of bricks, which brought an avalanche of coal down into the road. People rushed to pick it up, stuffing as much as they could into bags and even pockets and brief-cases.

All the time work was going on clearing the ruins, the rubble being used to build new houses. Little trains chugged through the streets at night taking it away, but the quantity was so great the problem arose where to dump it. It had been said by officials who were supposed to know that it would take at least twenty years to clear it but this prediction like many another was to prove false.

The housing shortage, still acute, was aggravated by the hordes of refugees daily pouring in from the Russian occupied East. To get a hold on the situation, bureaucracy grew and flourished, stretching out its tentacles in all directions . . . . forms, passes, permits to stay, permits to leave, permits for accommodation, permits to work . . Thud . . .Thud chorused the rubber stamps. The tyranny of the miniature robots dominated our lives too. For going on leave there were military exit permits, for returning; military entry permits; embarkation permits; disembarkation permits; meal tickets, in hostels; even bed tickets! Little mercy was shown if you failed to produce the relevant papers at the appropriate moment. You could be taken off the military train at a frontier; refused permission to board, or leave the ship; be left behind in some desolate spot while 'arrangements were made'. The Germans had a word for it — Stempelkrankheit — Stamp disease.

Living space for the 'Hamburgers' was strictly rationed — so many square metres per person. Outside every front door, a list of small white visiting cards as long as your arm. At night it was eerie to see flickering points of light emanating from the ruins where people had managed to build little brick igloos for themselves.

Even while thousands were still homeless the Germans, hankering often their beloved Kultur, were busy reconstructing and reopening the theatres, art galleries and concert halls. Although inevitably there were some grumbles it was generally recognised that people needed facilities to enable them to escape from the daily round of misery. The play being staged in a small theatre in Luneberg on the famous Heath could hardly be described as cultural enrichment. It was of all things, 'Charlie's Aunt', in German, 'Charlie's Tante'! We decided that would be too good to miss, and it certainly came up to our expectations, sounding even funnier in German than it does in English. The 'Aunt' played his role with uninhibited gusto, much to the delight of the audience. Loud bursts of laughter, cheering and shouts of 'Bravo' punctuated the performance. One of our party had thoughtfully brought a bottle of gin, and during the interval we went backstage to present it to 'Tante'. The second half of the play, as might be expected, proved even more uproarious with Tante reeling about on the stage, taking a swig at the bottle whenever his lines eluded him. Never again did I hear such sustained laughter from a German audience but then the boyish jokes in 'Charlie's Aunt' bring back the child in everyone, and the play has been translated into most of the major languages. Altogether, a hilarious experience, and who knows, maybe more 'uplifting' in those grim days than many an established classic.

The next day, wandering on the Heath, we arrived at the site of the monument erected by the allies to mark the spot where Germany formally surrendered her land, sea and air forces.

One couldn't help thinking that, after winning probably the greatest and most terrible war in history, the victorious countries might have been expected to put up an elaborate boastful sort of memorial on German soil but nothing could have been more restrained — just a plain slab of rectangular stone set in the middle of a little patch of scrubby grass encircled by a looped chain fence of the kind one sees guarding a park flower-bed, or suburban garden. At one corner a small white notice board ordered, 'Keep off the grass!'

On his return from a sponsored trip to the USA, as part of the American re-education programme for the Germans, Franz, full of enthusiasm for the new world, decided we ought to have a series of programmes about life in America which, he said, would certainly appeal to young people, many of whom had relatives over there, and ever since the war there had been a growing interest in everything American.

"I guess they shouldn't always hear what you call standard English," he said. "They should have a chance to hear that funny language, American-English. So we'll get Americans to play the characters. Do you know what really startled me in America?" he went on, seizing the chance as usual, to digress, "The advertisements. They are so funny. I remember the first that caught my eye, it was an enormous picture of a girl wearing only er — how do you call it? — Bustenhalter."

"A bra!"

"Yes, only a bra on her top half, and the slogan said in huge letters about a foot high . . . .

'Not Nature's gift, but so and so's lift!' "

That word Bustenhalter, literally a holder of busts, always strikes me as being typical of many German nouns, self-explanatory and direct — no euphemism required!

Franz went on chuckling. "You know America has the world's largest coffee cup, a lighted sign in New York harbour. It's forty-two feet high and could hold a million cups of coffee, if it could hold anything, and I liked this one, 'A funeral that'll make your family happy!' Can you imagine that in Germany?"

"Hardly," I said. "Now, these American programmes. It's a swell idea kid, but there's just one snag, I've never been to

America. I would have to write in an entirely new idiom and you know what Oscar Wilde said, 'The British and Americans have everything in common except their language'."

"Well," Franz said, "he was always trying to be clever. Anyway, it's not true. It may not be the English of your Kings and Queens, but it's still English, just a bit different."

"But I don't see how I can write these scripts."

"We know you can do it, lady. Just use that wild imagination of yours. Go to the American Consulate, talk to people there and find out about things that would be of interest. Get the facts and then just write a story — fiction based on fact. We'll call the series, 'Getting to know the USA'."

To Franz it was no problem. Being a capable script-writer he could have certainly done it himself. It all seemed rather vague. Such a challenge would require stretching the imagination to its limits, straining to put myself into the shoes of all kinds of Americans; men, women and children; from truck drivers and policemen, to professors and students. How would they talk and act in specific situations invented by me, taking place in a country I had never even visited? But then I had invented the characters too. So there were no holds barred. Although intensely hard work, it caused less strain than I'd anticipated and I managed to produce a series of plays with titles as diverse as 'A Drug Store', 'Thanksgiving Day', 'Adventures of a New York Taxi-Driver', 'The Drive-in Movie', 'Crossing the Hudson by Ferry Boat', 'Cowboys of Today' and many more, projecting what I could only imagine and hope to be the American life-style.

Americans in Hamburg employed at the Consulate, business men, and officials of one sort or another, together with their wives and children, even though few had any acting experience, were delighted at the prospect of displaying their talents as amateur radio actors, and there was no shortage of talent. The recordings were produced by tripartite co-operation; American actors; German technicians and producer; and an English script-writer. Naturally in my efforts to write what I thought was authentic American dialogue, I would sometimes slip up. One mother thought it advisable to reprove me, and with a trace of indignation, said:

"You know our children don't always call us Mom and Pop,

they say Mummy and Daddy just like English children.''

Another time, when writing a script about family life in a small American town, I had to think up a name for the place. Suddenly it shot into my mind — Flatbush! What could be a more unlikely name than that? but . . . .

"Say, whatever made you choose Flatbush?" asked one of the cast as we were making the recording.

"I invented it. You don't mean to say it's a real place?"

"Sure it's a real town," he said. "I've been there."

Uproar in the studio!

I came to the conclusion that no place names you could think up however fantastic, could possibly be as bizarre as those already existing in the States.

The German technicians constantly expressed surprise that high-ranking officials should have so little regard for their position and self-esteem, that they were prepared to spend long evenings taking part in little plays for schools, and doing it with such obvious relish. James Pease, a distinguished singer with the Hamburg Opera Company, used to come to the studio direct from rehearsal where he'd been singing The Flying Dutchman in the Wagner opera to speak a few lines as a truck driver or sheriff. A big burly chap, with a booming voice, the engineer had continually to remind him to stand further back from the microphone. "Herr Pease, kindly try to remember you are not the Flying Dutchman now!" he would say. "You are a New York taxi-driver, chewing gum." These evenings were always good fun. When the recording was finished the cast would troop into the control room to listen to the play-back, after which there would be a moment of suspense as everyone looked to the producer, hoping for the vital word "Verkauft" — "Sold"! It was all right and "in the can". We would then finish the evening off with drinks in the canteen.

I shall never get used to the extraordinary fact that the only characters and events in a radio play are those in the mind of the listener and, before they got there, in the mind of the writer. Seeing nothing, the listener yet has a clear picture of all that is happening, or rather not happening! and this experience is often powerful enough to generate strong emotions. Even now after years of writing and producing radio plays I find it an effort to try to visualize the true situation — nothing more than

D

people in a studio standing or sitting around a microphone reading from scripts. With no conscious effort except that of listening, the picture gradually begins to take shape. Perhaps this phenomenon is best summed up in the remark attributed to a small boy when asked which he preferred, television or radio plays. "Radio," he said, "because the pictures are better."

The American series entitled "Getting to know the USA", was on the whole being well received by students and 'eavesdroppers' to the schools' programmes; many being agreeably surprised to find that with a good basic knowledge of English, they had less trouble in understanding the American variety than they had imagined, having much exaggerated the small differences. Some teachers even said they found the pronounciation easier than standard English.

The Americans also appeared to be satisfied. One of the Vice-Consuls showed me an article he had written for a US Information Agency, headed 'Radio tells Germans about America', with a photograph of the American cast, Franz and me standing around a microphone. The same chap could not get over the fact that, although I was writing about the US, I had never been there.

"Would you like a trip?" he asked one day. I said I would like nothing better. "I know an air force guy who might be able to fix it. He's at our air-base, Ramstein. I'll tell him about what you're doing, and give you a letter of introduction. There's going to be a big military parade there soon. A new general is arriving to take command of the base. I'm fixing up with a party of German journalists to fly down and report. They'll be flying in a US military plane. I'll get you the papers. Just describe yourself as a journalist, and you can go down with them and stay the night at the base. We'll find you accommodation."

The evening before the trip he rang me. "Be at the airport at 7 a.m.," he said. "Slacks and parachute."

"Just a minute, what do you mean?"

"Bring your own slacks, we provide the parachute," and he rang off.

I spent an uneasy night, disturbed by frightening dreams.

"Jump!" shouted a gruff voice. A sudden push and I was hurtling down like a meteor, the wind whistling in my ears.

As usually happens, just before hitting the ground, I woke up. Well, next time at least I'll have a parachute! I comforted myself.

I arrived punctually at Hamburg airport at the dreary hour of 7 a.m. in the morning, wearing ski trousers, the only slacks I possessed, and wished fervently that I *was* going skiing. To my dismay I found that I was the only woman in the party. On presenting ourselves we were given a form, stating rather ominously that in the event of accident, death or injury the US would bear no responsibility, and asked to sign. There wasn't much cheer around and the Germans looked glum. Neither did the plane, a small propellor-driven machine, offer any comfort — no fully automated stewardess, no well-upholstered seats, no food, no drink — just two long metal benches facing each other, with small round hollows to accommodate your backside. The captain, striding down the gangway, smoking a fat cigar, ordered us to put on the parachutes, explaining that it was an army regulation for all military planes carrying civilians. The men didn't seem to have much difficulty, helping each other in what seemed to be a complicated operation. They took it all seriously, no laughing or joking.

But where to start? That was the question for me. After several frantic attempts to unravel that bewildering maze of webbing and straps and somehow get inside it, I gave up and sank back into the 'bucket' seat. If the worst should come to pass I would have to make the jump without a chute in a fit state to open, or stay where I was, the only passenger to go down with the crashing plane, and that heroic passenger the only woman. It would provide the reporters on board with a story guaranteed to be given front page treatment that is, if they managed to survive the drop.

''I'll give you a hand, Ma'am,'' said the grinning captain. He appeared to be deriving some entertainment value from my plight. The two rows of men sat facing each other silent and expressionless. No one gave the slightest hint that he could see anything funny in the situation. I didn't feel exactly euphoric myself. As so often in an aeroplane during the wait for take-off I had a strong urge to race down the gangway, fling open the door and like a rabbit released from the trap make a dash for freedom, powder-puff tail bobbing for joy.

"Stand still!" ordered the captain. He might have been saddling an intractable horse as he patted me on the flank and hoisted the pack onto my back, deftly fastening and checking the harness, a procedure mildly embarrassing for me but evidently all good clean fun for him.

"That's it, Ma'am, next time I guess you'll be able to fix it yourself."

'Next time!' I wished there'd never been a first time.

The captain then stood up in front, and between cigar puffs delivered a lecture on how to use the chutes should an emergency arise, endeavouring with some relish to turn us into the consistency of shaking jellies. He related a series of gruesome stories about what he'd known to happen, concluding with an account of an incident when a parachutist did the splits in mid-air and had to complete the descent fixed in that unhappy position. Audience reaction to this facetious patter was nil.

With the bulky pack on your back it was impossible to relax; you had to sit hunched forward in a most uncomfortable posture. Shortly after take-off we ran into a thunderstorm. A flash of lightning shot through the cabin and the little plane bucked like a rodeo horse. The young man next to me said nervously that he thought he'd pulled the rip-cord of his chute by mistake, and did I think he should inform the captain? "I will not be able to open the thing", he added ashen-faced. He was feeling ill and I gave him one of my travel-sickness pills. At least it might have the effect of making him too drowsy to notice whether the chute opened or not. I decided it might be a good idea to take one myself.

When we landed at Hanover the captain told us that because there would be an hour's wait we could get out and go to the airport restaurant for refreshments. Hurriedly discarding their chutes and looking decidedly more cheerful, the others tumbled out of the plane. I could perhaps have managed to release my chute but then before take-off I would have to put it on again. I hadn't got the nerve to ask anyone to stay behind to help — certainly not the captain! So I waited in my 'cold bucket seat', abandoned and forlorn trussed like an oven-ready turkey.

After landing at the base we were escorted by armed guards

to our huts on the compound. The base was an imitation of a small American town with large supermarkets, schools, football pitches, a church, and a conglomeration of nissen huts and aircraft hangars. The streets had names like Hollywood Boulevard, Lexicon Avenue, Broadway and so on. In the evening we joined the service wives and families in a bingo session. The prizes were luxurious, hair-dryers, crates of groceries, washing-machines, movie cameras and radios; none of them won by anyone in our party; but for the Germans it was an insight into at least one aspect of American life.

The next morning we attended the parade held on the airfield. There were military bands, marching and countermarching, inspections, speeches from the out-going and in-coming generals. Parked around us were scores of fighter planes; all could be airborne within three minutes, we were told. The war had ended but the fear remained.

My interview with the air force commander turned out to be rather unsatisfactory. He said it might not be all that easy to fix up an Atlantic flight for a civilian in a military transport plane but he would let me know. He then ordered Scotch on the rocks for us both. It came as no surprise when I received a letter from the commander regretting that he had been unable to fix me a free Atlantic flight in a US transport plane, but he sure hoped I would make it one day.

About a year later, I felt that if I was to go on writing the plays, I really should experience the American 'way of life'. I flew direct from Hamburg to New York and spent a wonderful month, 'action-packed', as the travel brochures like to put it, sightseeing and gathering material for scripts. Predictably, Franz remarked that the plays I wrote before the trip were better than those written after! I didn't see it that way myself, having gained a great deal from meeting and talking to all kinds of men and women, besides being able to see at any rate a little bit of the country. In the future I would no longer be forced to rely entirely on my imagination, which would mean considerably less effort.

Some people, when they heard I had been in the habit of writing about places without having firsthand knowledge of them, would get quite hot under the collar. Once when having drinks with a friend the conversation turned to my job.

"How dare you?" he shouted at me. "It's deceitful, morally wrong."

"Well, many distinguished authors have done it. What about H. G. Wells? To my knowledge he was never on the moon, but he wrote dramatic, and I believe, accurate descriptions of the moonscape in *The First Men on the Moon;* and isn't it the same thing with all art? I haven't heard that Turner was ever actually shipwrecked, but when you look at his paintings of shipwrecks you can almost hear the storm and feel that you are watching helplessly as the ship keels over, and the sailors throw up their arms and drown. You see, it's all in the mind! I think that the borderline between 'being there' and 'not being there' is pretty narrow, and even if you have actually visited the place that you are writing about, your account isn't necessarily a truthful one."

My flak had scored a direct hit. He snorted and returned to the bottle. End of a beautiful friendship!

In the English series for students entitled 'Scenes from Daily Life', I continued to write plays based on situations in which I had never found myself. If I had dramatized only my own experiences, the view of 'daily life' presented would have provoked yawns of boredom. Surely even my pious boozy friend couldn't fail to agree with that!

Not unnaturally, in a closely knit mixed community like the CCG, romances flourished; sometimes culminating in weddings. These were usually celebrated at the Church of St. Thomas a Becket. Since 1612 there has been a British church in Hamburg.

Of the many CCG weddings I attended, I recall particularly one rather subdued affair. Due to a power cut half-way through the service, the organ stopped abruptly, staying out of action for the rest of the ceremony. Sad and somehow all wrong that, instead of coming away to the triumphant accompaniment of the 'Wedding March', the new young husband and wife should have to start their first walk together side by side down the aisle in total silence.

Afterwards I thought we should have done something, anything rather than tolerate such an anti-climax, and it occurred to me that had this drama been one of my radio productions, I would have got up and made an effort to wield the congregation into a massive joyful choir.

The CCG Padre, a rugged outspoken Australian, was a popular figure and welcome guest at parties and receptions, which he never missed if he could help it. As an ex-naval man and organiser of the Mission to Seamen, he spent much of his time visiting British ships in port. His van, portraying on either side an elongated silvery angel about to take off, was a familiar sight in Hamburg. It seemed slightly incongruous and I used to wonder what the sailors made of it. Disconcerting, too, when telephoning his house to be greeted with, "Flying Angel here" announced in a gruff male voice!

The Sunday morning church services were generally well attended, being a lively social occasion like the getting together of a large family. After the service we would disperse to each other's houses or mess for drinks, and with luck you would be asked to stay to lunch. Anything was better than remaining in your own mess. Sunday, far from being a dreary day for people on their own, was something to look forward to, and for me a good day to make contacts and do a little talent spotting.

Even in the days of non-fraternisation, Germans were not barred from the services, and a few came regularly. Why they should come in preference to attending their own church was hard to understand, possibly to hear and practise English.

One good lady who always managed to be stationed directly behind me had an acutely penetrating voice, combined with a slight speech defect, being unable to pronounce the letter R. During the lengthy *Magnificat* exhorting all things to 'Bless ye the Lord, Praise Him and Magnify Him forever, Sun and Moon, Fire and Water' and so on, I was forced to endure through to the bitter end this shrill voice proclaiming over and over again, 'PWAISE Him and magnify Him "fowever", PWAISE Him and magnify Him "fowever"'!

When at last they were able to start rebuilding, brand new churches began to rise, ascending ever higher above the squalor down below; their tall slender spires piercing the thick grey layers of Hamburg sky, each a symbol of the rebirth of faith and hope after the 'Katastrophe' that had befallen their city.

Part 3

The Hamburg Opera House, badly damaged during the war, opened its doors even before major repairs had been completed. Accompanied by a German friend, eager to see a contemporary English opera, I went to Benjamin Britten's 'Peter Grimes'. Throughout the long evening pieces of roof pattered down around us like hailstones. Now and again we had to duck to avoid being knocked out by larger bits of debris but such is the devotion of Hamburg opera lovers, that even if the roof had been lifted off by hurricane Edna they would, I am sure, have stuck to their seats mesmerised by the troubled voice of poor Peter Grimes.

Shakespeare's plays, both in the German translation and in English, performed by visiting companies from Britain, were certain to attract large and enthusiastic audiences. We found the German acting less restrained and more declamatory than the English style.

Sitting uneasily through Hamlet in its entirety — four hours with only one five minute interval, and no refreshment — proved to be more of an endurance test than an evening's entertainment, especially as, from that great mass of words, we could detach only one coherent sentence — "Sein oder nicht sein" which, we decided, just had to mean "To be or not to be". After the first two hours my exhausted companion, also non-German speaking, confessed that he would rather "not be" at least, not where at the moment he happened to be!

It wouldn't have been so bad if Hamlet, a skinny middle-aged actor, hadn't ranted and raced through his speeches as though afraid the curtain would fall before he'd had time to finish and drop dead.

It was all too much for three British soldiers, who, clearly growing restless, gave vent to their boredom in uncouth bursts of laughter, usually during the more solemn moments. This was tolerated, everyone knowing what soldiers are, but a counter attack of furious 'Shsss' came when the intimate scene between Hamlet and Ophelia was greeted by a chorus of wolf whistles and smacking kisses. The shock wave rippling through the auditorium would have registered on a seismograph.

Theatre-going was not to be approached in a casual manner. Latecomers would be refused admission until after the end of the scene or act, and once inside complete silence was expected; no chatting, munching or shuffling about in seats.

During a performance of Goeth's 'Faust', regarded as almost sacrosanct, I happened to say something in a low whisper to a friend. Immediately a phalanx of heads turned on us in a concerted 'Ssssh', with the effect of creating more disturbance than my original modest whisper.

In the field of entertainment, comedy perhaps not surprisingly seemed rather thin on the ground, and farce non-existent. I had the feeling that humour was something to be locked away in a cupboard, brought out like a best suit of clothes, only for special occasions. It doesn't lighten the daily work load to the extent that it does in Britain. None of that cheerful banter and mild horseplay which does so much to humanise dull routine in, at any rate, the less dignified offices. No jokes, not even an occasional slap on the backside for the typist; that sort of thing was kept filed away till after office hours.

Once I summoned up courage to try out a home-made joke in the office. It was customary to keep the bare floors and staircases in a permanently highly polished condition. 'Vorsicht!' warned the notice — 'Frisch Gebőhnert!' — 'Freshly polished!' However, accidents were fairly common, it being not unusual to hear that Herr Braun, or Frau Schmidt was laid up in hospital with a broken leg or fractured arm, having fallen downstairs or slipped on the floor.

It was after one such mishap that I tried out the ill-fated joke, remarking to a colleague, "Frisch Geböhnert! is Germany's new secret weapon, isn't it?"

"Bitte?" he said, staring at me blankly. Well, it wasn't a very good joke and in the circumstances perhaps not in the best of taste.

During the First World War it was rumoured that the German High Command had to attend a course to study and analyse 'The English Humour' in order to gain a better understanding of the enemy's psychology. A story circulating in England related that they had reprinted the famous cartoon showing two British soldiers in a trench, staring over the parapet at an enormous crater. One is saying, "Cor, what made that 'ole, Bill?" "Mice!" replies his mate. The caption in German read, "But of course it wasn't mice, it was a shell." Probably a good old British gag, but on the right lines.

Now and again I came across a similar kind of ultra logical thinking. I had written a radio script in which the central character, although a scoundrel and a crook attracted everyone with his old-worlde charm. After typing the script the secretary handed it back to me saying, "I like the story but I do not understand why you called it 'Such a nice gentleman!' He wasn't nice and he wasn't a gentleman." Not easy in English or German, to explain — it was meant to be ironic.

Franz, however, did not fit into any recognised pattern. His colleagues regarded him as something of an eccentric. They were puzzled by his habit of debunking what he thought pretentious and pompous, and his apparent delight in shocking. The numerous conferences we had to attend were not events likely to raise the spirits, or stimulate exciting ideas. Dreary and boring, they were conducted in a solemn atmosphere; the delegates sitting stiffly around the walls as if in the dentist's waiting-room. When he wanted to speak a delegate would put up his hand, waving it about like a schoolchild. Little dialogue, or exchange of views took place, only a series of speeches — usually far too long. Possibly the explanation lies in the fact that during the past years discussions, committees and conferences were not the accepted way of determining policies. There had always been someone to make the decisions and give the orders.

At one of these affairs, a teachers' conference, I happened to be sitting cross-legged, gently swinging a foot to and fro, its shoe dangling from my toes when, during a particularly tedious discourse by Herr Doktor so-and-so, Franz seized by one of his mischievous impulses, delivered a sharp kick to the shoe, sending it flying across the room to touch down at the feet of one of the more elderly gentlemen. The Herr Dr. abruptly halted his flow of words in mid stream, while all eyes focused on the wretched man, struggling in an agonising dilemma. What should he do? Pick up the shoe, cross the room and with a low bow and heel-click hand it back to me, or simply try to pretend he hadn't seen it? He decided on the latter course, but things didn't seem quite the same again.

I felt sure that later the incident would be described as 'Unerhört' — unheard of, or a little stronger — a word often bandied about when condemning some especially disgraceful incident. "And Herr Reinholz in his position — unerhört!"

The German film industry, had not yet got into its stride and most of the films were British or American. Imports of the old Charlie Chaplin films always went down well, but we were curious to see what the audience would make of Charlie's satirical view of Hitler and his grandiose schemes in 'The Great Dictator'. For most of the time, except for some incredulous gasps and a few half-hearted laughs, there was silence. Even the masterful scene where Charlie as Hitler, dances and juggles with a globe of the earth and his monologue in gobbledygook German, failed to draw much response. We found it rather a depressing experience and felt we had to restrain our own laughter. Could it have been that around the figure of Hitler there still lingered an aura? To laugh would be irreverent. You don't laugh at a god, even a dead one.

If only at the start of Adolf Hitler's rise to power there had been a voice bold enough to declare that the emperor had no clothes. Of course we knew there were people less gullible than most who didn't like the way things were developing and formed protest groups, but in the beginning they were simply not numerous or powerful enough to root out the noxious spreading weed. If only there had been more people with a sense of the absurd, prepared to use all the means at their

disposal; caricature, satire, jokes; to cut down to size and mock
this ludicrous posturing figure. If only Germany had produced
a Charlie Chaplin — would it have worked? Or would the little
fellow have found himself in a concentration camp?

The four of us — two men and two girls — agreed, that had
we realised the full extent of the horrors awaiting us, we would
not have gone within a hundred miles of the cinema. It was
showing the films taken by the Nazis themselves inside their
concentration camps. That they had camera men actually on the
spot recording the atrocities, appears to indicate a complete
absence of shame or revulsion; even a kind of pride in the
'work'. The films had been discovered by the allies while
examining the archives. Whether the decision to exhibit them
to the public came from the allied or German authorities I have
no idea, but it was surely the right thing to do. There were
those who believed the stories and pictures had been fabricated
by the allies, and dismissed them as hate propaganda. One
might have anticipated that the people would stay away, but
something, perhaps curiosity, impelled them to go. The cinema
was full. At last they were brought face to face with the ghastly
reality. Had they known what was going on in the camps? —
'Camps' — what a misnomer — or hadn't they? Obviously
there must have been some unaware of it all, and others who
knew everything; either because they were present in some
capacity, or because they had played a part, however small, in
the business of extermination — a very big business indeed.

Certain scenes remain branded on the mind for ever — the
guard snatching an apple from a starving boy; long queues of
naked people squashed together being herded into the gas
chambers; people driven like cattle to market, shoved into the
open trucks of the death trains; jackbooted women guards
swinging dead bodies from side to side to gain momentum as
they hurled them into the already full pit; the camera proudly
focusing on the trade mark A.J. Toph & Sons over the ovens
of the crematorium; the shaven skulls and striped pyjama type
uniforms; the great mounds of boots and shoes and human
hair; the stick-insect people, and people not like human beings
at all, just crawling skeletons, scrabbling vainly in the earth for
food.

Emerging from the cinema the Germans moved slowly as if

sleep-walking, silent, grey-faced, vacuous. Some leaned on each other's shoulders weeping openly. As for us, we wanted only to escape from the darkness into the light of common day; to run round the lake; to breathe good clean air; to have a drink; to do anything sane and healthy — anything to obliterate the tormenting images. I think for the first time in this country we had all felt a wave of hate rising, seeking to burst out and vent itself on anyone born a German, unmindful of the fact that many of the victims were themselves Germans.

"Nazi bastards!"

"Christ!"

"The sods!"

A futile reaction but . . . . nobody could think of anything else to say. Stunned out of our wits we just sat drinking in silence.

Some of the war crimes' trials were taking place in Hamburg. One of those in the dock was General Manstein. Stripped of his military trappings, he looked, what presumably he was, just a tired old man. More interesting characters were the two women concentration camp leaders; the younger, the notorious 'Black Angel'. Wearing good fur coats and heavily made up, they frequently turned to grin at each other, now and then exchanging scribbled notes. From their brazen demeanour throughout the long indictment, one had the impression they wondered what all the fuss was about. The proceedings were extremely lengthy; the interpreters having to translate from the German every few minutes. Behind me sat three British girls in CCG uniform. To my amazement I saw that they were actually knitting, and appeared to be completely indifferent to the continual recital of horrors. They brought to mind, unreasonably of course, the hags of the French Revolution, glancing up from their clicking needles only to watch the guillotined heads fall.

What do the new generations, the children grown up since the war, think and feel about the infamous Nazi regime and the crimes for which many of their parents were responsible?

It is my belief that more than all the outpourings of politicians, newspaper articles, film documentaries, television programmes and pages of statistics; one little girl, Anne Frank, has directly brought home to young people the real implication of Nazi crimes. With the discovery of her diary in the attic of the Amsterdam house in which she and her family took refuge from the Nazis; a normal intelligent child was revealed; a blameless human being personifying the murdered masses; a teenager with whom the young could identify; not a statistic; not just another Jew to be liquidated — but Anne *was* a Jew and she *was* liquidated in the Belsen concentration camp.

The young people made a martyr of her, and the Anne Frank cult was born. Many taking wreaths with them, went on pilgrimages to Belsen. Her diary has been translated and published in most, if not all the major languages. As if writing to a friend she begins each entry, "Dear Kitty". She relates with good humour the small happenings in the confinement of their daily lives — writes about her school friends and others she knew. To Kitty she confides her innermost thoughts and feelings with never a trace of bitterness or anger at the cruelty of it all, only a deep longing to enjoy the ordinary life of a normal child.

Two American playwrights took her story as the theme of a play, 'The Diary of Anne Frank'. It was staged in a Hamburg theatre. There we are in the Amsterdam attic with Anne and her family. Linking the scenes is the small figure of Anne seated alone in the centre of the stage, a single spotlight on her as she writes up her diary, the words relayed through the loudspeakers in the auditorium. Throughout the play the suspense is almost unbearable. The family knows, and we know that sometime, anytime, the knock on the door will come, the knock that tells them they have been discovered. When at last it comes the curtain quickly falls. From the audience of predominently young Germans arose a deep despairing groan.

Anne and her family were discovered in August 1944. In March 1945 Anne died in Belsen — just two months before the liberation of Holland. She was fourteen.

For most people in the cities, food was still the biggest worry, with few signs of improvement in supplies. After the war a system of rationing had been introduced, but it never really worked. The rations, unlike those in Britain, were simply insufficient to keep body and soul together. So the black market together with bartering took over. The situation however, was uneven. A very big discrepancy existed between stocks in the Russian zone and the Western zones. Sections of the British press maintained that the Russians were using food for political ends, because there was enough to spare in their zone which should have been coming to Western Germany. The real trouble was that Humpty Dumpty had had a great fall and no one wanted to put him together again. Instead the four giants, having pushed him off the wall, now had him cut into quarters so that each could have a piece for himself. It was said that the British had the industry, the Russians the food, and the French and Americans the scenery. But part of the blame for the shortage of food in our zone lay with the farmers who preferred to look after themselves rather than supply their fellow men. Along with the manufacturers they were still waiting for the allies to introduce the currency reform, which would bring into being a brand new Deutschmark instead of the worthless Reichmark. Until then they would continue to barter their food for something of real value.

At the main railway stations, the trains, crammed with people inside, and outside on the roofs and buffers, still left every day for the country where grandmother's diamond necklace and gold rings, precious heirlooms, antiques and valuable paintings would be exchanged for a pound or two of potatoes, eggs, butter, vegetables to be stuffed into sacks and brief-cases.

The Aktentasche — a kind of brief or document case — appeared to be an indispensable article to every German, whatever his trade or profession. Doctors, drivers, teachers, office workers, building workers, plumbers, tramps, school children, like business men going off to the city, all carried in one shape or form an Aktentasche. From my observations while sitting on park benches, watching the world go by, it contained anything but documents or papers; generally a few slices of black bread; maybe some bruised apple windfalls; a handful of home-made biscuits together with bits and pieces scavenged from our dustbins. The Aktentasche concealed it all with dignity. Where these universal carrier bags came from was a mystery. You couldn't go to a shop and buy one. I acquired mine from a derelict character in exchange for a packet of 'Players'.

By this time I had managed to get accommodation in a different mess — a mixed one — in a street called Innocentia Strasse, an address guaranteed to provoke ribald comments. Here I had a large, rather empty room to myself. Everything was in shades of brown, yellowish brown walls, muddy brown wardrobe, shiny dark brown linoleum, a shabby brown leather armchair, all that remained of the original furniture. The best thing was the large open fireplace. I used to go out and collect as much wood as I could carry back. Visiting German friends would bring armfuls of sticks with them so that we could have a roaring fire in the evenings. Out would come the drink ration and the good old Naafi fruit-cake.

Inevitably at some time the conversation would turn to politics, and it was interesting to hear the other view of recent happenings. One of my German colleagues actually claimed that Germany was not to blame, because by issuing an ultimatum to Germany, Britain had started the war. During Anglo-German discussions I was to hear this extraordinary assertion again. Such distorted 'reasoning' ignoring the invasion of Poland, always brought on a mood of despair and a longing to pack my bags then and there.

On the whole I tried to prevent political arguments from developing, thinking it wise to let the past go.

From the beginning it had been decreed that the Occupation Forces should not take any food from the German land, the reason being that the people needed every scrap for themselves — not an egg, not a cabbage, no potatoes, not a lettuce — nothing. All our rations were imported. The bread baked by the army was as full of holes as gruyere cheese; the bakers obviously taking pride in finishing off every loaf with a crisp black crust. The weekly egg came with Sunday breakfast. The daily butter ration was no bigger than a walnut. There was no fresh milk; fish and cheese were almost unknown, and there was no fruit. In fact, the rations were far worse than those in Britain. Vegetables, unrationed at home, were either dried onion or dried cabbage. Surely the mastermind who devised a method of dehydrating cabbages could never have had fun munching his way through the end product, which resembles a handful of stuff you might offer a friendly horse looking over a gate.

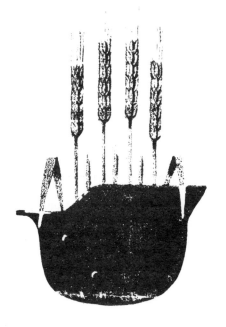

GERMANY
under control

*Pamphlet issued by British Military Government
before the end of the war.*

E

HAMLET
PRINZ VON DÄNEMARK
Trauerspiel in 5 Akten von Shakespeare
Übersetzt von A. W. v. Schlegel

In Szene gesetzt von Alfred Noller

Bühnenbild und Kostüme: Caspar Neher

Claudius, König von Dänemark... Bernhard Minetti
Gertrude, Königin von Dänemark
und Hamlets Mutter ....'......... Eva Fiebig
Hamlet, Sohn des vorigen und Neffe des
gegenwärtigen Königs .... Will Quadflieg
Polonius, Oberkämmerer .... Willy Grill
Laertes, Sohn des Polonius ...... Helmuth Ziegner
Ophelia, Tochter des Polonius .... Hanna Rucker
Horatio, Hamlets Freund .... Heinz Klingenberg

Voltimand ⎫ ⎧ Kurt Groth
Cornelius ⎪ Hofleute .... ⎪ Peter Homfeld
Rosenkranz ⎬ ⎨ Wilhelm Walter
Güldenstern ⎭ ⎩ Omar Leutner

Osrick, ein Hofmann........ Hans Conrad Goesehe

Marcellus ⎫ Offiziere ...... ⎧ Joachim Hildebrandt
Bernardo ⎭ ⎨ Herbert Gärtner

Francisco, ein Soldat .... Willy Wiesgen
Ein Matrose .... Karl Fleischer
Reinhold, Diener des Polonius........ Carl Sartory
Der Geist von Hamlets Vater...:...... Gerhard Bünte
Fortinbras, Prinz von Norwegen.,... Dieter Stürmer

Schauspieler .... ⎧ Joseph Offenbach
⎨ Karl Fleischer
⎩ Alexandra Wehrtmann

Ein Priester.................... Heinz Suchanthe

Zwei Totengräber .... ⎧ Hermann Kner
⎨ Willy Wiesgen

Mit Genehmigung der Militärregierung

Actual size of programme due to paper shortage.

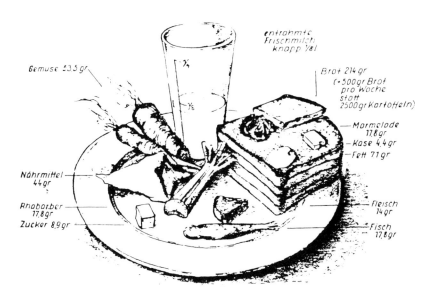

The German daily rations from a German newspaper.

This is washing day in Essen.
Amidst the fantastic devastation in the Ruhr, life somehow continues.
But it gets worse, and Europe suffers.

Lack of food and fuel drives people to the black market.
Here German looters jump on to a stationary train and seize coal.

US Information Agency News

Radio Tells Germans About America

USIS Hamburg: Help is given in preparing programs on American life which are broadcast over the Northwest German Radio network to several thousand German school children. Left to right are Assistant Information Officer Mason C. Dobson, NWDR script-writer Georgiana Melrose, Radio School Director Franz Reinholz, Film Officer Laura Gnagi, and Information Officer Wilbert B. Dubin.

Christmas lights reappear as Hamburg rises again.

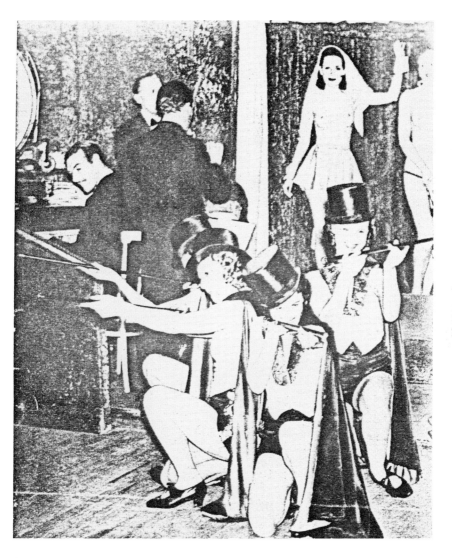

Nazi magazine illustration purporting to be a scene in a London nightclub — Girls "shooting" at the German enemy.

The author — Hamburg, 1947.

A few of the British in the mess undoubtedly had dealings with the black market. One chap, a naturalised German and a doctor, used to come down to breakfast holding in front of him about a quarter of a pound of butter stuck on the point of a knife, and under hostile glares dump it onto his own plate. For Sunday lunch there was usually a scraggy part of an anonymous animal which was quite uneatable. For some unfathomable reason I had been elected food member, which involved keeping an eye on the rations and dealing with complaints. Bob, as we called the young German house manager, would bring in his sad travesty of a Sunday joint at breakfast time and ask despairingly, "Frau Melrose, what shall I do with this?"

When I could bring myself to look at the object, I'd tell him, "Do what you like with it, only take it away."

We had our suspicions that Bob indeed did what he liked with our rations, for we seldom got even what we were entitled to; but it was difficult to prove anything, and in any case, the rations were simply not worth getting steamed up about. The German staff used to express surprise at the poor quality of our food. They had obviously expected that, like all conquerers, we would live off the fat of the land, taking what we wanted and treating ourselves to the best of everything. Fortunately, we were able to supplement the rations by having meals in the various Naafi clubs and restaurants, but of course these had to be paid for, and even here there was a dearth of fresh food. Being an 'other rank', I wasn't entitled to eat or drink in an officers' club, but was allowed to use only the warrant officers and sergeants' mess. However, this regulation quickly became part of my collection to be scrupulously ignored.

Some of the most luxurious hotels and restaurants in Hamburg had been commandeered by the various British organizations, the NAAFI, Church Army, YMCA, and so on. The internationally famous Atlantic and Four Seasons Hotels by the lakeside, had become officers' clubs. It was rumoured that, long before the end of the war, the army had planned the take over, and ordered the RAF to drop their bombs elsewhere. The YMCA had chosen a fashionable restaurant, formally specialising in oysters. The elegant decor remained unchanged, not so the menu with the ubiquitous bottles of HP sauce, and of course, egg, sausage and chips.

We were lucky to have some charming maids in the mess, who had clearly known better days, but appeared to be entirely without grievances. To every two or three of us there was one maid. Gretel and Annie, the nicest of the lot, looked after me. They would do anything for small rewards. If I had been able to get a length of dress material from England, Annie would run it up in two shakes for a packet of Naafi tea and a piece of soap; and Gretel did all my washing and mending for more or less the same. It was remarkable how they always managed to look clean and smart, like Victorian maids in black dresses with little white aprons. Another more elderly woman liked to practise her English. I never heard her speak German. She used to address the men as, "My, Sir", following logically the German form of address, "Mein Herr", and after every question or remark she would tack on, "Isn't it?" "A fine day isn't it? Another cup of coffee for my sir, isn't it? More coffee for the lady, isn't it?" Her name was Gertrud, but inevitably she was always called "Isn't it".

The diet, with its lack of fresh vegetables and fruit, naturally had an adverse effect on our health, resulting in frequent minor complaints. These were dealt with — one hesitates to say 'treated' — at the Army Medical Centre; a down to earth, no nonsense place, unconcerned with such 'non-essentials' as sympathy and patience; which I had the misfortune to discover for myself.

"Please can you deal with this?" I asked the medical orderly, indicating a Vesuvius-like eruption on my jaw.

"Where's your 253/487/910?" (something like that) he asked. None of your smooth, "Well, now, what's the trouble?" But then I suppose the 'trouble' was fairly obvious.

"My what?"

He repeated the list of numbers. Then, seeing me still dazed, he said impatiently, "The form of course. I can't do nothing without that."

"But I've only got a boil."

"It doesn't matter what you got. I got to have the form. There'll be some in your mess."

So off I trotted to the mess, returning with the completed

253/487/910. I found it puzzling why the army was so keen to know your religion until a fellow patient set my mind at rest. It was, he said, because in the event of your death, they could organize the appropriate type of funeral. The centre did nothing to strengthen one's faith that soon all would be well. In the bare drab room, a decrepit old woman in worn slippers was leisurely sweeping up fag ends, empty cartons and other more unpleasant debris, piling the muck into little heaps. With each stroke of her broom, small clouds of dust rose and fell, causing her to explode in paroxisms of coughing, or perhaps she had TB.

Having fixed a makeshift dressing the orderly said, "I'd better just test this," and he plunged it into a basin of steaming water. Then rolling up his sleeve, he carefully placed it on his hairy chimp's forearm before slapping it on to my jaw.

These days I can imagine that the makers of one of those documentary programmes, to whom a scandal in the Health Service is meat and drink, would seize on this little incident for the subject of a 'full and fearless investigation'. Without doubt my reception at the military hospital would also come under the scrutiny of the media, and be given the full exposure treatment. Suffering belatedly from measles I was delivered there, in dressing-gown and slippers, by official Volkswagen taxi. My heart went out to future passengers in that taxi.

On arrival, I had to join a queue for reception, the tail of which was in the open, and it was raining.

"What's yer name?" demanded the corporal who appeared to be in charge.

"Melrose."

"What's yer first name?"

Wait for it! I told myself.

"Georgiana."

"What?"

"Georgiana."

"Ow do you spell it?"

Laboriously he entered each letter on the form, screwing up his face as if in pain, continuing through the standard list of questions, religion, of course, next of kin, maiden name, and a dozen or so more. By this time with a soaring temperature I was feeling close to death, my only consolation being the thought that with every heavy breath myriads of little red spots were busy traversing the ether from me to him. It was a relief to find myself at last in splendid isolation. I'd had visions of being confined to a ward populated by bodies suffering from a diversity of interesting complaints, all freely available for swapping, measles perhaps for chicken pox, and scarlet fever maybe for typhoid. As the hours drifted by I began to feel abandoned, left to pass away from measles; when abruptly the door burst open and in with the wind strode a large army sister. Slapping two flat white pills down on the bedside table, she barked, "Bash on with those," and was gone with the wind without even giving me the chance to tell her with my last gasp that I'd never felt less inclined to bash on with anything!

The highlight of the hospital routine was the colonel's inspection. In preparation for this solemn rite, a great deal of to-ing and fro-ing took place; nurses and orderlies milling around like ants, dusting, tidying, and putting away every object in sight. The bedside table was swept clear. Even the curtains were taken out of their restraining loops, straightened and made to hang at attention.

"Now we've got to straighten you out," said the nurse, drawing the bedclothes so tight that I was forced to lie rigid as an Egyptian mummy. "Don't move again," she ordered rather unnecessarily.

Slowly the colonel advanced, escorted like a tribal chief by fawning attendants, junior doctors, matron, nurses, sisters. On reaching my solitary bed he peered down as if examining a mysterious bug under the microscope. "H'm, very spotty," he commented, and that was all from the great man.

It reached my ears that every patient was supposed to get a tot of whiskey before lights out. When I complained to a nurse that, on several occasions, mine hadn't arrived, she said reasonably, "Well, if you didn't get it, someone else must have had it." Against such logic further argument would have availed nothing.

Treatment at the Army Dental Centre followed the same basic pattern with which I was becoming depressingly familiar. It boiled down to the absence of things we normally take for granted; the formidable chromium appliances, the spotless basin merrily gurgling away, the methodically arranged tray of instruments with a white uniformed nurse at hand; the only appliance on view being the intimidating chair in the middle of the room. The tooth had to come out said the dentist, but it seemed reluctant to do so. After much pulling, wrenching and muttering under his breath, the dentist had a bright idea. Visibly recalling how power was generated in his college tug-of-war team, he placed a knee firmly on my chest and, leaning his weight backwards, expended the last ounce of all that brawn. Out the thing shot, spattering us both with a horrid mess.

The next time I had tooth trouble, a colleague at the radio station recommended a German dental surgeon who had somehow managed to restart his practice — and a pleasant contrast that was — surrounded with what, at any rate, looked like up-to-date equipment in a hygienic atmosphere; he wore a clean white coat, and did the work with great gentleness.

"What do I owe you, Herr Doktor?" I asked.

"Please, Frau Melrose, do not give me marks," he said. "But, if you can manage it, a tin of sardines and a piece of soap for each stopping."

Almost as much as food, people coveted soap. Many attempts were made to create substitutes. One method had something to do with soaking potato peelings; but none seemed to be really effective.

More than a year after the capitulation, it was still a mad financial world, with bartering and cigarettes taking the place of currency. It was really most peculiar how cigarettes had become a fetish and a currency to the extent of being passed from hand to hand until they were no longer fit to smoke. On the first occasion that I smoked in the street I was followed by a trail of men, women and children, waiting to pounce on the stub as I threw it away. I took only a few puffs before dropping the cigarette, and did not look back.

Soon after my move to the Innocentia Strasse mess I did a rash thing. I 'adopted' Jürgen, an eleven-year-old German boy. The maids had told me about him. He was always hanging around the house, kicking stones in the street and picking over the dustbins. He looked half-starved and they suspected he was sleeping rough. My reaction, I suppose, was like anyone elses would be, "Oh, poor little Jürgen!" Then, on an impulse, I'd said, "Well, tell him he can come up to my room whenever he likes. There'll always be the Naafi cake and biscuits."

Jürgen lost no time in accepting this invitation out of the blue. The next evening when I got back from the office, he was there standing in the middle of my big brown room. I hadn't foreseen communication problems, but my German was obviously a foreign language to him, and his dialect just as obscure to me. We managed with a few basic words, 'cake', 'biscuit', 'drink', 'more', 'go', 'come', 'tomorrow'. He crammed large hunks of cake into his mouth, and appeared to swallow biscuits whole like a hungry dog. To get rid of him I had to take him by the hand, lead him to the door and almost push him out. He clearly imagined the invitation would include bed and breakfast.

Every evening when I got back from work he would be there, standing, waiting. His solemn dark eyes followed me everywhere like the eyes in some portraits seem to do. It wasn't long before I began to resent his constant presence, while feeling uncomfortably mean for doing so. I wished he wouldn't come any more. I wanted my room to myself but I hadn't the heart to tell him. Then one evening he wasn't there, nor the next, nor the next. The maids hadn't seen him. They thought he'd probably been picked up by the police and taken to a refugees' home. So many sad children like him. Who stole their birthright to play, laugh and shout for the joy of living? The god of war stands in the dock.

Recovery from defeat was terribly slow. It was estimated that Germany was minus probably as many as seven million men, about one half killed, and the other half in prison camps. Obviously nothing could be produced by under nourished people who had to spend the day foraging for food. The country was just dragging itself along, confused by our policy of destroying potential war machinery, and the problems created by the artificial boundaries. Regular incomes, pensions etc., were non-existent for most. People were trapped in a vicious circle. Until industry could be restarted, there wouldn't be the money to buy food; and without sufficient food people couldn't work in industry. To prevent widespread starvation some food was being imported from Britain, paid for by the taxpayer, a state of affairs which from time to time provoked angry comments in the press.

'DO THE GERMANS NEED OUR FOOD?' was the title of an article by John Gordon printed in the *Daily Express* of 30 June 1946. A report by another journalist carried the headline, 'MUST WE CUT OFF OUR NOSE TO SPITE THE HUN'S FACE?' in which he demanded a more positive plan for reconstructing and organizing all available labour in the British zone to get the country back on its feet; concluding, 'Weeds grow on rubbish heaps, but never flowers.'

Nevertheless, amid all the gloom and criticism, there were items to be entered on the credit side of the account, even though many seemed perhaps more negative than positive. Compared with the conduct of armies of occupation in the past, such abstract qualities as lenience, tolerance, lack of wholesale vengeance, were surely not to be disregarded. We did not rob the land to feed ourselves. No longer did any Jew, so-called traitor, or poor deranged creature have to lie sweating with terror at the tramp of approaching jack-booted feet, and then the knock on the door in the night.

Part 4

Controls were relaxed sooner than many had expected, and responsibility gradually handed back. We permitted a press with a degree of freedom; encouraged the setting up of local government; got the schools and universities reopened; all of which gave hope for the future. However, at the same time the Germans resented the cavalier manner we were taking over hotels, castles, country houses, villas, and sports clubs and, more than anything, they resented the destruction of factories considered to have war potential, and the continuing blowing up of shipyards.

Sometimes the conscientious weeding out of Nazis was carried to absurd extremes; a second violin in the radio symphony orchestra barred because it had been discovered he'd held a job as a minor clerk in the Party, and the suspension of a young girl for failing to admit membership on the Fragebogen, the dreaded questionnaire which everyone applying for a job had to complete.

"Under Hitler we had to be Nazis or we got into trouble," people were saying, "Now we have to be anti-Nazis or we get into trouble."

Poor old Germans! Their world had been turned upside down and, for that matter, ours wasn't quite the right way up either. In yet another article in the *Daily Mail* — the date 23rd July 1946 — Alexander Clifford had claimed 'We're teaching the Germans to hate democracy.' A German joke was going

72

around . . . "Well, how do you like democracy? Are you being warmed by the democratic sun?"

"Yes, but it's funny, it turns some of us red and some brown again."

Many of us realized that in certain quarters, justly or unjustly, the CCG was becoming a laughing stock. We had our own views — CCG (BE) — British Element, stood for Complete Chaos Guaranteed (By Experts), or Charlie Chaplin's Grenadiers and, alluding to dealings in the black market, Cigarette, Coffee Government.

Meanwhile we continued to live within the artificial confines of our own society, just as the British did in the cantonments of India, having little contact with the natives. My friendship with Franz and others at the radio station was dismissed in the mess as 'fratting', and considered to be mildly eccentric behaviour.

It must have been impossible for the people at home to form a clear and truthful picture of the conditions in our zone, neither could anyone comprehend the magnitude of the problems and difficulties. In any case who cared about the Germans? The war was over and there was trouble enough picking up the pieces of your own life and starting again.

In this abnormal and, to me anyway, depressing environment, the British set about enjoying themselves. Hardly an evening went by without a party. No reason or excuse for a celebration was needed. Parties became almost automatic, each mess taking it in turn to throw one. If you couldn't stand the pace and the drink you had to decide which to go to, but most people went to the lot. One mess party was indistinguishable from another, with identical Naafi loose covers and curtains, even glasses and crockery, not to speak of the same old faces, same old jokes and funny stories. The consulates, of which there were a great many, also from time to time gave parties, or receptions, as they preferred to call them; the Americans being the most lavish in hospitality; none of those tiresome bits and pieces on little sticks, or small squares of soggy toast, but a large table spread with delicious goodies, sometimes a whole roast turkey and a couple of chickens, and we'd be invited to cut off slices for ourselves, and of course all this washed down with a plentiful supply of 'Scotch on the Rocks'. It was satisfying, literally, to be able once in a while to enjoy such a good meal. No wonder the uninvited would resort to gatecrashing.

These parties were a happy hunting-ground for me, continually on the lookout for fresh talent to take part in our American radio programmes. Vice-consuls, their wives and children were all willing to have a go. To the German technicians and studio staff it was astonishing that so many British and Americans who had never spoken a word into the microphone, or set foot on a stage, could give a performance that wouldn't disgrace a professional actor.

Easy winners in the party stakes were the receptions held on board visiting ships of the Royal Navy; the officers courteous and distinguished in their becoming uniform, and the sailors always smart and attentive. To receive the gold-embossed invitation card your name had to be on a list at the British Consulate. We had an idea that it was compiled by one of the typists during the tea-break, or perhaps the office boy. Anyway, I always managed to go, if necessary, by tagging on to friends.

A crowd of curious Germans would be standing on the quay to stare as, in full evening plumage, we marched up the gangway. One felt blown up like a VIP or 'star of stage, screen and radio', but Hamburg being a great port, the real stars they'd come to see were the British ships. The aircraft-carrier *Victorious* was so vast it was hard to think of her as a ship; she seemed more of a place. As each guest stepped on to the flight deck an officer boomed out his or her name to the assembled company .."Mr James and Mrs James! Mr Hopkins and Miss Brown!" When incredibly he bawled, "Lady Chatterly!" It's my guess the navy was silently praying he would add, "and her lover!"

A sailor was detailed to show anyone interested around the ship. To move at all involved clambering up and down innumerable perpendicular ladders, at the same time having to concentrate on holding down a skirt. Loosen your hold for a second and a blast of air blew it up to the waist, presenting the grinning sailors with an unexpected, though possibly not unwelcome change of scenery. It's hard to conceive of a more unlikely venue for a cocktail party than the interior of a submarine. Surrounded by an awesome tangle of pipes and intricate machinery, with not an empty square inch on which to place a glass, useless when stuck with a boring fellow guest to remark casually, "Oh please excuse me, I've just spotted old so-and-so, I must have a word with him." You just had to stay put. The captain and controller of all this gadgetry could have been mistaken for an eighteen-year-old schoolboy, but was in fact twenty-three, much younger than many members of his crew.

To one who, when momentarily confined in a lift, has to be restrained from breaking down the door, it is baffling that anyone should choose to earn a living working for long periods in a narrow steel tube deep under the sea.

The garden party at the British Consulate was an annual affair to which every Tom, Dick and Harry received an invitation. Whatever the temperature outside one particular consul insisted on driving us into the garden. Like a fierce mother goose with wings outstretched, he would hiss "Shoo . . shoo . . " and wait until we had all ambled out reluctantly as children into the bleak playground. The band thumped out the standard old pieces from 'Lilac Time' and 'The Gondoliers'. Waiters glided between bushes balancing trays of sherry and 'White Ladies'; and finally the toast to the Sovereign — if you were lucky — first, it was round and round the mulberry bush to capture one of those slippery creatures, a waiter bearing the ultimate treat, a glass of champagne.

The consulate used to lay on a reception for every visiting VIP, and a constant stream of them converged on Hamburg — bishops, professors, actors, musicians, politicians — if, at the reception, you had any big ideas about meeting these great ones face to face so that for years after you could indulge in a little 'name-dropping', you were more than likely in for a disappointment. 'Walkabouts', mingling with the proletariat, had not yet been thought up. The VIP usually migrated to the centre of a mini solar system, surrounded by a ring of satellites, effectively barring intruders from outer space.

The academics had as a rule been invited to lecture. I found it puzzling why many of them paid little regard to the fact that the audience was made up of Germans to whom English was a foreign language, which many hadn't heard for years. They would gabble, use jargon and pretentious speech. I attended a lecture given by the poet, T.S. Eliot talking mainly about his own poetry and thought it odd that such a brilliant man should not have been able to put on a better performance. With head lowered he read his talk in a monotonous tone, never once varying the inflexion. I got the impression that the audience had not understood a single word, which was sad for they must have come eager to hear what the great man had to say, and gone away with a sense of frustration.

It often seemed the more erudite the speaker the more dreary and boring his lecture.

Sometimes visiting speakers got more than they had bargained for. If at the end of his talk a lecturer was rash enough to invite questions from the audience he could occasionally find himself flummoxed. In the pause following a long discourse by an elderly professor on Nineteenth Century English Literature, a lady suddenly bounced up, "Please, can the Herr Professor tell us how the English make custard?"

Wiping an imaginary custard pie off his face the professor stammered that regrettably his ignorance of this domestic operation was total, and he would have to ask his wife.

Sooner or later the visitors (not the bishops) would almost certainly express a desire to sample the less lurid pleasures of the famous Reeperbahn in the suburb of St. Pauli, known as Die Grosse Freiheit — 'The Great Freedom', because there 'anything goes'; striptease, bars of every sort, nudes in and out of bubble baths, women wrestling in mud, men masquerading as women, and vice versa, endless permutations on the theme of 'cabaret', 'blue movies', and girls, girls, girls — girls displaying themselves behind lighted windows, for sale like any other merchandise. During slack periods 'shoppers' would watch them knitting, or doing some cosy domestic chore.

Periodically the authorities used to order 'clean-ups' but nothing much would change, at least not for long. However, you could have a perfectly respectable and amusing night, if that's what you wanted.

The 'popular' newspapers in Britain were now working themselves up into a lather over the CCG. Reporters arrived in droves and, after tasting the heady delights on offer, returned home chockful of righteous indignation to produce articles which generally contained a few grains of truth embedded in a mass of extravagant verbiage. Eye-catching and startling headlines blazoned their way across the pages . . . . "BRING HOME THESE MEN!" "CORRUPT, LAZY, THEY DESCREDIT OUR RULE!" *Daily Express* — 4th September 1947.

"The Control Commision includes far too many maggots feeding on the corpse of defeated Germany," writes the reporter, going on to describe what he says is a picture of a typical Control Commission Officer, whom he calls Civilian Officer Spiv. This Spiv chap has bought himself a Volkswagen for £160, or maybe managed to wangle a requisitioned Mercedes to use for 'swanning', that is disappearing for days on some nebulous expedition using petrol and rations provided by the accommodating British taxpayer. There follows a lot more about the bungles of Spiv. He is alleged to have ordered hundreds of gallons of anti-freeze for Volkswagens when everyone in his right mind knew the vehicles did not use water, but were air-cooled. Other gaffes the report continued, included the order for a number of fishing boats to be destroyed because they had been built two feet longer that the official specification.

'GOOD TIME MINORITY MAKE GERMANY A PLAYGROUND!' ran another headline, and continued . . . "Less than 400 miles from the shores of England there is a dreamworld peopled by Britons, a careless place of little work and endless play, of nylon stockings and French perfumes, of unlimited drink, music, dancing and night-long parties. The flashy set, crowd the great hotels and luxurious nightclubs of the British zone. Long-haired young men, sleepy-eyed women, usually in heavy furs and chunky jewellery". . . and a great deal more in similar vein designed to cause the poor wretches in austerity-ridden Britain to foam at the mouth with rage and envy. "Officers' clubs", the reporter explains, "provide their 'entertainment'. One such club, 'Tobbacco King' Reemtsa's million pound dream-house outside Hamburg, must be one of the most ostentatiously, lavishly luxurious establishments of its kind in existence."

It was true that this large country house had been taken over for our leisure use, and renamed predictably The Country Club. The 'Tobacco King', Reemtsa, had meanwhile been condemned to a more restricted life-style behind bars. To us the 'dream-house' was as welcome as a lush oasis to a desert traveller, and I certainly had some good times there without so much as one twinge of guilt; enjoying even Naafi tea in the beautiful grounds; the indoor swimming-pool with its bronze statues of naked Aryan supermen; Saturday evening dances under the ornate chandeliers in the ballroom. At one of these I was introduced to a grey-haired naval officer calling himself a Constructor Captain, who simply loved dancing — the old-fashioned sort — especially the waltzes. Unfortunately his wife didn't share his enthusiasm. However, she had no objection to his being partnered by other women. An excellent dancer, he never tired, and by late evening or early morning his partners were barely able to stagger off the floor, but, to echo Eliza's song in 'My Fair Lady', 'I could have danced all night' — with him!

At the tennis club, oddly enough, I had met another naval officer in a similar predicament to that of the captain. He was a vice-admiral, mad keen on tennis, but his wife wasn't interested. Catching sight of you sitting alone with a drink recovering from a strenuous three-set match, he would pounce and rush you off for a fierce game of singles. He was small and agile, and compensated for his lack of strength by playing a rather mean game, frequently popping the ball just over the net. I, being too lazy to run, he usually beat me much to the satisfaction of his wife, always present watching placidly. A big stout woman who, when out with her husband, usually waddled about ten yards behind him, reminding one of a rather heavy ship being towed along by a bustling little tug.

Beggars were frequent callers at the mess and 'married family' houses. Most had fled from the Russian zone where, according to the familiar stories, they had been forced to work, starved and generally ill-treated. Now, free in the more liberal West, they could survive only by begging or stealing. Many were little more than children. Usually they asked only for bread — "Just a piece of bread" — but later when conditions began to improve some grew bolder, presenting a list of demands. One night I opened the door to find a teenage boy who thrust a bit of paper into my hand on which was scrawled, 'No bread, only cigarettes and coffee.'

From time to time there appeared on the front door, minute

symbols resembling Egyptian hieroglyphics. I didn't discover what they meant until, calling on a friend for tea, I caught a ragged old tramp in the act of marking the door of the house. Out of curiosity, I enquired what he was doing. As far as I could understand, it was a 'beggars code'. He grinned and said in so many words :

"This means 'Good, you'll get something. The lady always gives me cigarettes.' A sign like this means, 'Don't bother. Nothing doing'."

On returning home I scrutinized our door, observing with some satisfaction that we had been awarded, a 'favourable' mark!

In the more serious British newspapers, much was being written which examined in depth the policy of re-education in the British zone.

"Chances in the Moral Education of the Germans that we have missed," was the theme of an article by Lt. Col. the Hon. C.B. Birdwood. Others, equally unhappy about the standard of the occupation demanded that more should be done to attract the right kind of people "in order" as one writer put it, "to wean the Germans away from their lack of respect for the individual, lack of sense of personal responsibility and muddled hysterical thinking." There was no sign of this being done, he said.

Meanwhile with the approach of Christmas, the CCG rank and file was more concerned with the business of party-going and party-giving than with matters of moral education; each mess in the throes of organising a party for German children, complete with all the trimmings, a decorated tree, sweets and cakes and of course a Father Christmas with a sackful of presents.

One day, passing my old mess, I ran into Supervisor Bridget.

"How are you getting on in the new mess?" she asked.

"All right, thanks, the food's no better."

"Are you still learning German?"

I had been putting in a few periods of free time studying, what Mark Twain called 'The Awful German Language' ever since I'd arrived. After learning the first week's lesson in *German for You*, I concurred absolutely with Mark Twain: the structure of the language is awful.

"Yes," I said to Bridget, "I'm plodding on with it. Why?"

"Well, we're having this Christmas party in the mess for German kids, but we can't find a man to play Father Christmas. You see, we must have someone with at least a smattering of German so that he can speak to the kids like a friendly old man."

"You're not asking me? You can't have a female Father Christmas!"

But Bridget insisted, saying nobody's boy-friend was willing to air his German in public, and time was running out. "You can pitch your voice lower and try to sound a bit gruff. Anyway, under all that gear they won't see much of you." The red cloak and hood had arrived from England, she continued, the costume belonged to her Uncle Fred who had regularly played Father Christmas when she and her brother had been small children. "Of course we knew it was him because he had a funny smell, but we didn't really mind." She prattled on, and finally I agreed. It seemed rather mean to say no when she'd gone to so much trouble, and the children had to have their Father Christmas. I started to swot up a few appropriate words to say to them.

On the day of the party I arrived early and changed in Bridget's bedroom. She showed me the long white beard, a fine set of whiskers and even bushy white eyebrows she'd made out of cotton wool; altogether a most effective disguise.

"We thought it would be much too tame if you just came through the door," Bridget said. "So we want you to knock on the window and come in that way."

The room was on the second floor, with at least a sixteen foot drop outside that window to a sort of concrete well below, fenced off from the road by a row of spiked iron railings. I didn't much like the look of it. However, Bridget had got it all worked out.

"We've borrowed a ladder and all you have to do is climb up on to the ledge, it's quite wide. Then at about six o'clock knock loudly on the window. I'll open it and you'll jump in with your sackful of presents. It will be a terrific thrill for the kids."

All went according to plan. As I crouched on the stone window ledge, not more I guessed, than about fifteen inches wide, I could hear the din of chatter, squeals and shouts created by about forty small children enjoying themselves. I knocked loudly on the window. A sudden silence descended as Bridget flung it up. Jumping into the room, I announced in the gruff tone I'd been cultivating and, I should think, an unmistakably English accent, "Hier kommt der Weihnachtsmann!" — Here comes Father Christmas! — With the children surging around, I drew the little presents out of the sack, handing one to each. No one had thought to tell me it was a German tradition that, before receiving his present, the child should recite a short poem. Some wouldn't even accept the present until they'd said the poem, which made it a very protracted business indeed, and after each one I had to think of something different to say, variations on "Dankeschön", "Dass war sehr nett", "Dass war wunderbar", and anything else I could wrest from my limited German.

Finally, when all the presents had been distributed, I said, not without considerable relief, "Auf Wiedersehen, Kinder!" and the chorus came back, "Auf Wiedersehen!"

Pushing the window up I climbed through, and Bridget pulled it down behind me. It was a dark cold night with a few desultry snowflakes drifting down. I twisted myself round for the descent, lowering a foot to feel for the top rung of the ladder — nothing — the foot was waving about in space. Turning round again I looked down, and went stiff with horror. The ladder had gone. Reviewing the situation I decided the one thing I could not do was to go back through the window into that room full of kids. Such an anti-climax would spoil the party. They might even expect a second round of presents. I did the only thing left and shouted for help — in German — "Hilfe! Hilfe!" in my normal voice.

One or two passers-by looked up, and in the dim light of the street lamp patently thought they were seeing an apparition in the form of a Father Christmas perched on a ledge and, shaking their heads in disbelief, hurried on. Just when I thought my toes woud start to drop off from frostbite one of the maids from the mess came out, shouted something, disappeared and returned with a man carrying a ladder. Everyone seemed to think the party had been a great success, even though one little girl was heard to remark suspiciously, "Father Christmas had

G

long white hands.''

Bridget inquired what I was doing for Christmas, which was only two weeks away. I told her I didn't know. We were entitled to a free trip to UK, but the weather was bitterly cold and the thought of that long and dreary journey acted as a strong deterrent. We had to be called at four-thirty a.m. to catch the leave train, which rambled across most of Germany on its way to the Hook of Holland where we spent the night in a transit camp nissen hut, embarking the next morning on the military ship to Harwich. If the crossing was rough I would be seasick all the way. To make matters worse 'other ranks' did not have cabins, only hard bunks somewhere down below. From Harwich the journey continued by boat-train to Liverpool Street. Then I had a further train journey home.

"Why don't you come to Berlin?" Bridget said. "I'm meeting Jack there and we're staying at the Naafi Club. We could all go around together."

"That sounds a wonderful idea, but won't I need papers and passes, etc.?"

"Yes, but you know people in education. Get someone to make you out papers for a conference or something."

As it happened, an educational conference was scheduled to take place in Berlin shortly before Christmas, and because I was already working in education, I had no trouble in getting the official papers, and was commended for wishing to attend.

The windows of the unheated train were completely frozen up, the glass opaque with frost. My fellow traveller in the sleeper, a big strong-looking youngish woman dressed smartly in khaki, introduced herself as an Australian journalist, and said her assignment in Berlin was to report on various aspects of life (should there be any) in the city.

I had been hoping to get a good night's sleep, but that woman was in no hurry to go to bed. Standing in front of the mirror she began to remove her make-up, dabbing, patting and massaging; studying her face from every angle. After about a quarter of an hour, satisfied that all was in order, she unpinned her bun, letting the straight brown hair fall to her waist, before starting to brush it with vigorous sweeping strokes.

"Can't we have the light out?" I said, getting more and more irritated.

"I always give my hair a hundred brush strokes before I go to bed," she said, "and I've got seventy-five more to go."

It was a relief when she finally settled down in her bunk below me and put out the light.

Sometime during the night we were woken up by a loud banging on the door.

"Everybody out and up to the front of the train!" shouted a soldier. "This coach has caught fire underneath. Hurry up and go to the front."

Flinging on some clothes I jumped out of the bunk. The Australian got up languidly and started to put the previous operation into reverse, slowly and deliberately applying make-up and then brushing out her hair once more. It looked like being another hundred strokes. A tramp of boots, and in marched the sergeant.

"Aren't you ready yet, Miss? There's no time to do all that. We're in the Russian zone. We may have to leave this coach behind and you with it if you don't get out."

"Miss indeed! I'm a colonel," she muttered indignantly.

"Perhaps the sergeant didn't notice the pips on your nightie!" I remarked unkindly.

Interpreted — her withering stare ordered — 'Seven days confined to barracks for insulting a superior officer!'

Arriving at the Berlin station I was thankful to find a solitary taxi. In response to my loud taps on the window, a bundle of clothes draped over the steering wheel began to exhibit faint signs of life, gradually straightening up. On seeing a uniform the man clambered out and sprang to attention. I gave him the address of the Naafi Club and we set off through the near empty blackened burnt out city.

"Where are all the Russians?" I asked, expecting the streets to be swarming with fur-capped, jackbooted soldiers.

"Oh, it's much too cold for them," the driver laughed. "They'll be indoors."

At the club there was no sign of Bridget. "She left yesterday," the manager told me in answer to my enquiries. "She's gone off with that colonel friend of hers."

"Didn't she leave a message for me?"

"No."

"Do you know when she's coming back?"

"No, she said the colonel was sick and that he'd been ill ever since he went into Belsen with the army. He was one of the first in when the camp was discovered after the war, and he's never got over what he saw."

I felt myself sinking into a deep well of misery and self-pity. Alone for Christmas in this freezing ruined foreign city!

Going into the lounge after breakfast I observed two men in civilian clothes, and obviously British, seated at a small table.

"Just starting to think about Christmas presents," remarked the older man, who was tying up parcels with brightly coloured string, and we got into conversation. They had been attending the conference and had decided to stay on in Berlin for the holiday. After hearing my sorry tale, they invited me to join them for Christmas dinner, and any other festivities there might be; for which kind gesture I was truly thankful.

Naafi did their best with plenty to eat, including a traditional Christmas dinner, and more than enough to drink. Given the circumstances it turned out to be not at all a bad Christmas. Secure in our little haven of contrived gaiety we were glad to forget the scenes outside; scavengers in the streets, and shadowy figures picking over our dustbins; but the spirit of Christmas in Germany is not easily dampened. From time to time there could be heard floating over the wasteland the haunting melody of 'Silent Night, Holy Night'.

The holiday over, it was back to work. Every week I was writing a script of one sort or another. Although from time to time we received letters of appreciation from teachers and children, especially about Henry and Barbara; I felt I was working more or less in a vacuum, and should have a better understanding of the problems at the receiving end — the class-room where it was all happening. It was decided that I should pay regular visits to schools, sit in the class-room with teacher and children and listen to the programmes, observing the reaction and joining in the follow-up discussion.

A good number, though not all schools, had by now been equipped with radio sets. Textbooks being in short supply, the school broadcasts, covering a wide range of subjects, including current affairs and news of other countries, were especially useful to teachers whose information about the outside world during the war years had been perverted by propaganda, much of which they now knew to be false.

The Germans presumed that anyone wearing a uniform of the occupation forces was a natural fund of information; in the same way, I suppose, that we trust our policemen to know all the answers. You had only to put a foot out of the door of the mess to be buttonholed by a wandering soul asking if you could tell him how to get to such and such a Strasse, or Platz. Even if I know the way perfectly well, I am not exactly quick off the mark in English when directing a stranger to some place or other. In German the process involves considerably more brainpower. Conscientiously trying to assemble nouns, adjectives and verbs, in their right order with correct genders, I would stand dithering on the pavement. Was 'Strasse' masculine, feminine or neuter? And what on earth was the word for 'crossroads', and 'turning'? 'Right' and 'left' were OK — 'recht' and 'links'. And when finally I had launched into my hesitating, halting spiel, the enquirer, growing impatient, would move away, shaking his head and muttering under his breath, with not so much as a 'dankeschön'! leaving me feeling distinctly aggrieved. After all, I had taken trouble and done my best.

In the future I resolved to my shame not to bother. Whether I knew the right answer or not I would just reply with the single word, 'geradeaus' — 'straight on', receiving in return a grateful 'dankeschön', and watching guiltily as my victim strode off confidently into the blue.

Now when I think of it I am overcome with remorse. How many hapless people have I done this to? And how many are still marching 'geradeaus'?

Rules about the wearing of CCG uniform were fortunately soon relaxed. The trouble was finding something else to wear. I certainly had no intention of visiting schools in uniform. I wanted the calls to be in a friendly and informal atmosphere, and a uniform, especially that one, would create the opposite effect. Fortunately, the Naafi dress shop had just got in some new stock, and there I acquired a cheap suit.

My first visit was to a school on the outskirts of Hamburg, to listen with a class of twelve year olds to a Henry and Barbara play. The building had been damaged at one end, but sufficiently patched up for limited schooling to carry on. However, nothing was easy, not even finding the place. Roads and tracks through the ruins were still few and far between and, to add to the confusion, street names with Nazi connotations like Hermann Goering, or Himmler Strasse had been changed to something more innocuous, although there was, and probably still is, a street called Adolf Strasse; named perhaps after a less infamous Adolf, or maybe an oversight.

The school, a forbidding red brick building with bare stone corridors and steps, gave an impression of overall greyness, unrelieved by any colour in paint or materials. After a welcome in his best English, the headmaster escorted me to the class-room. About forty children immediately sprang to attention, chorusing a well-rehearsed "Good morning, Missis Melrose".

They all looked well-scrubbed and neat, thin, but not unhealthy. The girls wore bright pullovers with skirts, and clean white socks. Most of the boys had on the traditional Lederhosen, leather shorts turned up at the bottom, with braces joined by a strap across the chest — very practical because as the boy grew, the braces could be lengthened.

The teacher, obviously nervous, had trouble tuning into the broadcast, and I was afraid we would miss the beginning. Then giving up, she called for Dieter, clearly the lad with 'technical' know-how. A little fiddling of knobs, and out into the class-room came the warm familiar tones of Henry, "Hello everyone, this is your old friend, Henry!"

A ripple of excitement ran through the class. The children smiled delightedly and some clapped their hands. Thereafter they listened intently to the radio play.

Barbara was going shopping. She asked Henry to take a cake out of the oven in half an hour's time. Later we hear the door open as she returns, sniffs loudly and says accusingly, "Henry, there's something burning!" The children shrieked and one or two shouted in English "The cake, Henry forget the cake!" I could swear the smell of that burnt cake penetrated all four corners of the class-room. Never underrate the power of illusion!

Talking to the children afterwards it was gratifying to find how well they'd understood and enjoyed it all.

Before I left the teacher told me they would like to sing an

English song which they had learned especially for the occasion. At a signal they all jumped to their feet and burst into, 'It's a Long Way to Tipperary.'

I found the little scene intensely moving. Only a short time ago these children had probably been spending the nights crammed into concrete bunkers, or deep underground, seeking refuge from British bombs.

I always looked forward to the school visits being sure of surprises. Once I was sitting with a class listening to one of my intermediate programmes. We had chosen as introductory music for the play, which was set in Scotland, Mendelssohn's 'Fingals Cave'. Afterwards, while discussing the play with the children, I said something about your great composer Mendelssohn who, on a visit to the Inner Hebrides, came away so impressed with the strange basalt columns that he felt inspired to write this music.

The children looked rather blank and, taking me to one side, the teacher said, "You know, they've never heard of Mendelssohn. Works by Jewish composers were banned by the Nazis." Feeling a bit shaken, I mentioned the incident to a colleague in the music department. He showed me a catalogue in which were listed the works of great composers. On the pages devoted to Offenbach, Mendelssohn and other Jewish composers, was scrawled the one word Jude — Jew. The works were burned, but after the surrender the members of the symphony orchestra produced the scores. They had buried their own copies in the grounds of the radio station.

Now and again there arose delightful misunderstandings in the use of English. With a class of teenage girls I was listening to one of my programmes in the series 'Famous People', which told the story of Grace Darling; dramatizing how the young heroine rowed out single-handed in a terrible storm to rescue men from a sinking ship. Later, when the teacher was questioning the children, a girl raised her hand and asked, "Please, what means a heroine?"

"That is easy," replied the teacher without a moment's hesitation. "A heroine is the wife of a hero."

Having no wish to embarrass him in front of the class, while at the same time feeling duty bound not to let this delectable gaffe go completely unchallenged, I could only murmur, "Well, not necessarily!"

The Henry and Barbara broadcasts nearly always produced enjoyable and surprising reactions. In one of the plays Barbara went out leaving Henry to do the housework. While he was vacuuming, the little girl from next door called and feeling sorry for Henry asked if she could help. Unfortunately, the only actress we could find to play this part was a girl of fifteen; although I thought her voice could pass for that of a child of twelve.

After the programme the teacher asked me to put questions to the children. They had obviously understood the story. Finally I said, "Somebody came round to see Henry and stayed to help him with the housework. Who was that?"

"Please, his other wife came to see him," a small boy replied promptly.

For the teachers and children my visit to the school was obviously regarded as a very special event. The head would say, "I've told them an English lady is coming and they are all very excited."

Occasionally, I arrived as the children were having a hot meal in class; usually a sticky porridgy concoction; and a child would be detailed to offer me a bowl of the stuff, which somehow I had to force down.

Even from the older boys and girls I never detected the slightest sign of hostility, only eagerness to speak English and put questions to me about life in England.

My script-writing took on a new dimension now that I could see in my mind's eye those children in school. Being new to the job, which I didn't really think of as work, I found it immensely stimulating that my invented characters should be so real to the German youngsters, bringing if only for a few minutes, some enjoyment and fun into the generally rather serious business of school. Perhaps in a small way the programmes would help to dispel any lingering feelings that we were the enemy.

For the teenagers and students, I tried in the plays to get across something of the flavour of daily life in Britain and America; family problems and attitudes; jobs; events at school; pets; sport; village life; and occasionally more demanding and complicated matters such as attempting to define in simple language what we mean by freedom of speech, and how democracy works at the 'grass roots' by committees, discussions and compromise.

Of course there were times when certain happenings in my scripts drew adverse comments but some of the criticism appeared to me rather petty. For instance, Henry sitting on the beach at Brighton, picks up a stone and throws it for Spot the dog to run after.

"But isn't that a bad example to the children?" I was asked. "The stone could hit someone."

And some of our favourite nursery rhymes came in for attack. Henry usually sang one at the beginning of each story, and the younger children loved to join in. All the same, our well-loved 'Three Blind Mice' was censured because, "It's cruel, isn't it? The farmer's wife cuts off their tails."

I suppose there is no answer to that, but it did seem a little curious coming from people whose classic fairy-tales by the brothers Grimm are hardly notable as examples of the milk of human kindness.

With changing circumstances the CCG was in a constant state of flux. In the office the major had gone to another job, and his place taken by a former head of London's Goldsmith College. The first thing he did was to get all three of us upgraded — himself, his assistant and me. I was promoted to Control Officer, Grade 3, and with it went a pay increase, on paper at least. It took exactly a year for the cash to percolate through the clogged up pipes of the Foreign Office machinery. I was still being paid my £4.14 a week as Billet Supervisor, Grade 4. However, now having acquired officer status, I could say goodbye to 'other ranks' and egg and chips in the Warrant Officers' and Sergeants' Mess, and join the privileged hierarchy in Officers' Clubs.

Those of us working in the educational and cultural branches of the CCG, whatever our qualifications and abilities, or lack of them, were expected to play an active part in the promotion of that indefinable product called the British Way of Life. For this purpose there existed an institute, Die Brücke — the Bridge.

I found myself with some misgivings participating in earnest Anglo-German discussions; brains trusts, poetry and play-readings, and even, when no other speaker could be conscripted giving chatty little talks on everything and anything remotely connected with the arts. My first talk was called 'Animals in English Poetry' with the actor who played 'Henry' reading aloud the poems. Research into this subject had revealed that there was hardly a multi-legged or even legless passenger in *Noah's Ark* which hadn't been chosen as a subject for verse. Blake's *Tyger, tyger, The Donkey* by G. K. Chesterton, *The Cow,* Robert Louis Stevenson, *The Rabbit,* Anon, birds in plenty, some sad lines about a pig and even one poem 'To a Worm'. What the audience made of it all we didn't like to contemplate. It probably reinforced preconceived notions that the British were mad about animals, or — just mad!

After this effort, to my dismay, I was invited to take part in a tripartite 'Women's Evening' discussion in German to be held in Amerika Haus, the American counterpart of Die Brücke. A German, American and Englishwoman were to discuss 'Women's Work in Society'. As the Englishwoman I would be representing Britain, all most alarming. To refuse would have appeared churlish. There was nothing to it but to do one's homework and hope for the best.

The chairman called on each of us to start with a little talk about the work of women in our own country. It wouldn't have surprised me to see members of the audience stuffing fingers into their ears to shut out the pain of my hideous English accent. It even hurt me. However, I rambled along explaining how women and girls had contributed a great deal to the war effort, working alongside the men in the Services and factories. My German, not being equal to any detailed elucidation of this work and, stumped for something else to say, I just wound up rather lamely with "Und so weiter", the German version of "And so on", or "etc.", which produced a totally unexpected effect. The audience rocked with merriment. Apparently the way I'd said it implied that all those girls' efforts could not in fairness be described exclusively as war work! Anyway, it produced, though unintentionally on my part, a welcome note of frivolity.

I thought the time had come to start learning German in earnest, and decided to take private lessons. Ursula, a girl I'd recently met, whose husband was still a prisoner in Russia, told me that her friend, a doctor of literature, would be delighted to give me tuition. And so Herr Dr Gerhard Braun came into my life. Three times a week, assisted by an endless supply of alcoholic drinks and cigarettes, we wrestled with the 'Awful German Language'. Gerhard was a smooth, very fit man in his early thirties. You could never have guessed that he'd fought in one of the fiercest battles of the war — the struggle for Stalingrad; was captured and taken prisoner by the Russians. The only physical damage he'd suffered was the loss of the top joint of a thumb. While in captivity he taught himself Russian, which he spoke fluently, as well as excellent English. Gerhard was determined that I should learn to speak German correctly, and disapproved of my reluctance to get bogged down in the sticky morass of grammar.

Having discovered while struggling to learn German on my own, that every noun was one of three genders, masculine, feminine or neuter, I soon decided that, in order to be able to speak without first chewing over in my mind which nouns had which genders, and then matching up the articles and adjectives, I would treat them all as masculine, which would simplify matters, enabling me to progress much more quickly. After all, supposing one became involved in a discussion about whether to employ a knife, fork or spoon for a certain dish, and you got the genders of these implements all wrong, people would probably still understand what you were talking about. In any case, how was it possible to remember the gender of every noun, especially when there didn't appear to be any sense in the distribution? In German, a young girl has no sex while a turnip has. In his amusing essay Mark Twain has fun translating literally a few lines of conversation he found in a German Sunday school book :—

Gretchen: "Wilhelm, where is the turnip?"
Wilhelm: "She is in the kitchen."
Gretchen: "Where is the beautiful English maiden?"
Wilhelm: "It has gone to the opera."

More infuriating examples: A tree is male, its buds are female, its leaves neuter. A horse is neuter; cats are female, tom-cats included; the sun is female; the moon is male; a knife is neuter, a fork feminine, a spoon masculine; and by some oversight of the inventor of the language, notes Mark Twain, "a woman is female — Die Frau — but a wife — Das Weib — is not; she is neuter, which is unfortunate." And the treatment of adjectives drives him up the wall. "When a German gets his hands on an adjective he declines it until the common sense is declined out of it." If we wish for example to speak of 'Our good friend' we stick to one form, and that's the end of it, but German having four cases it's not so simple, and goes like this : —

Nominative	—	Mein gut*er* Freund; my good friend.
Genitive	—	Mein*es* gut*en* Freundes; of my good friend.
Dative	—	Mein*em* gut*en* Freund; to my good friend.
Accusative	—	Mein*en* gut*en* Freund; my good friend.

And supposing the object of the friendship happens to be female, there is a variety of new distortions to be learned, and should you have a good friend who is neuter like a horse, or possess more than one good friend, you will have a further two sets of changed endings to memorise.

Comments Mark Twain. "Let the candidate for the asylum try to remember these variations. It might be better to go without friends in Germany."

There is also the maddening business of splitting a verb in two, putting one half at the beginning of an exciting chapter and the other half practically at the end. And what about those formidable compound words? Mark says that some German words are so long they have a perspective and cites the following : —

Freundschaftsbezeigungen.

Stadtverordnetenversammlungen.

"These things are not words; they are alphabetical processions. I take great interest in these curiosities and now have quite a valuable collection. When I meet another collector we exchange our newest specimens. Here are some more which I bought at an auction sale of a bankrupt bric-a-brac firm.

Waffenstillstandsunterhandlungen.

Unabhaengigkeitserklaerungen.

Generalstadtsverordnetenversammlungen."

My own first encounters with such monsters used to throw me into a state of panic, but once I had learned the secret of deciphering them they held no more terror. You simply split them up into their separate components, quite an enjoyable hobby.

The mildness and paucity of German swear-words is another source of worry to Mark Twain. "German ladies," he complains, "are constantly exclaiming, 'Ach Gott!' 'Mein Gott!' 'Der Herr Jesus!' I once overheard a German countess say to a young American girl, "Our languages are so alike. How pleasant to find that we say, 'Ach Gott!' and you say, 'Goddam!' ""

I could tell him that I have heard stronger swear-words, and on occasions employed them myself, especially over the matter of genders. I've also eavesdropped on street corner conversations conducted with the utmost economy, obviously getting somewhere without feeling the need for a single monster, and always found this most encouraging, for instance:—

"Nein!"

"Ja."

"Wirklich?"

"Ja, ja."

"Ach so."

"Na ja."

Among English friends I circulated the brochure of my own original language course, specifically designed to assist and encourage their efforts.

LEARN GERMAN IN ONLY TEN YEARS!!!
WITH NOT MORE THAN
TWELVE HOURS' STUDY DAILY!!!!

This exciting streamlined method of auto-instruction is completely attuned to the demands of the Space Age. Like a guided missile tearing through, and beyond the earth's misty atmosphere, the student will burst through the communication barrier to the soaring heights of Hoch Deutsch at a speed unparalleled in the history of foreign language teaching.

On terminating the first five years of study the conscientious student should find himself in complete mastery of the genders (der, die, das) and in a position to proceed to the work covered in the next three years, namely cases (nom. gen. dat. acc.). Skimming rapidly over these he will at the end of the eighth year be fully qualified to tackle Part II of the course — strong verbs (stinken, stank, gestunken, etc.), on completion of which in the tenth year he should be capable of meeting with aplomb any basic linguistic situation in West Germany (the East German language will be dealt with in another volume).

Should the student aspire to converse on an intellectual level, a further short decade of patient study will bring this laudable ambition within reach of fulfilment (Volumes II — XII).

Learn the language of Goethe and Goering! Hurry! Hurry! It's later than you think!

Below — a selection of letters from ungrateful students :—

Dear Sir,

After twelve years I've made no progress. Please refund my money.
Yours
"dissatisfied".

Dear Sir,

I did it in three months. It's a rotten swindle.
Yours etc.
"disgusted".

Disregarding my own language course, I made pretty good progress with Gerhard's tuition, even though he did insist on my going back to learning genders. An enthusiastic teacher he only flagged when there occurred a temporary absence of his indispensable teaching aids — whiskey and cigarettes.

During one lesson when they both happened to be in plentiful supply he suddenly asked: "How would you like to learn Russian?" and I gaily replied "Why not?"

I must have been out of my mind, and I didn't even have a drop of the hard stuff. Possibly Gerhard was anxious to show off and practise his Russian. Anyway, we started with one lesson a week, translating from Russian to German and back again with hardly a word of English, and soon I was regretting that absurdly impulsive decision. Before you could get anywhere, an entirely new alphabet of curious signs had to be learned. We continued the lessons sporadically for about eighteen months.

Now almost all that I can remember is that in Russian there is one word to mean both 'world' and 'peace', and the word for 'red' is almost the same as that for 'beautiful'; from which there must be something to be deduced. One or two comforting things can be said about the Russian language. It has only one form of past tense, and seems to manage perfectly well without the use of the definite or indefinite article which, after the pernickety German arrangements, came as a relief. In Russian you say: 'Put book on table', in the manner of blunt north country people, concluding that paltry little words such as 'the' and 'a' are just not worth bothering about.

There was a small colony of Russians living in Hamburg, mostly elderly people who fled to Germany to escape the Bolsheviks. Sprinkled among them were members of the aristocracy, dukes and counts, who before the revolution owned enormous estates, wielding powers reminiscent of feudal days. Now they were among the poorest in Hamburg, working at menial jobs and earning a few marks by giving Russian lessons; always hoping for a restoration of the Czars.

Gerhard invited me to go with him to one of their meetings so that I could hear genuine Russian spoken. I think he had a secret feeling that I suspected him of teaching me one of the more obscure Chinese dialects.

The meeting was scheduled to begin at seven-thirty. There were to be talks about Pushkin, for it was the hundred and fiftieth anniversary of his birth. He is regarded as the founder of all Russian culture. Over the lecture table, framed in green branches, was a large portrait of him. More than half an hour went by with no sign of the lecturers. A German-speaking Russian, the first to arrive, told us that in Russia if a meeting was arranged to begin at seven-thirty it really meant eight-thirty; everybody knew this and would turn up accordingly; and it was exactly an hour later that people began to troop in.

I hadn't expected to understand a word of the lectures, and I didn't. It could just have well been in Chinese, but it was wonderful to hear for the first time the richly flowing language. Looking around at the audience I saw that many were dabbing their eyes, recalling perhaps happier and certainly more prosperous times in their homeland. A melancholy reminder how many sad lives are wrapped up in that package neatly labelled 'The Refugee Problem'.

One evening my German friend, Ursula, arrived at the mess in a very disturbed state of mind:

"It's Hans," she said. "I've had a postcard from him. He's been freed. He's coming back to Hamburg on Saturday. He wants me to meet him at the station with some warm clothes. He says he's got nothing."

It was the first time that Ursula had heard from her husband since he'd been taken prisoner in the war on the second front. She hadn't known whether he was alive or dead, and in the meantime she and Gerhard had been living together. It was the classic situation, the plot of innumerable books and plays, the prisoner in his cell dreaming of the day when he'll be free and return to the cosy little nest where his loving young wife will nurse him back to health and they'll resume their happy life together. But the young and lonely wife has sought consolation with another man. Then it's the job of the playwright, or novelist, to decide how things will work out; but here was Ursula having to face the real thing, and her feelings were ambivalent. Although relieved that Hans was alive and free, she knew his home-coming could break up her life with Gerhard. Nevertheless, she had already absorbed the shock and made her decision. It was unthinkable that after his long years of suffering he should come back to nothing and, perhaps because he himself had been a prisoner in Russia, Gerhard at once agreed they could not let that happen.

"Of course I'll be there to meet the train. There'll probably be several hundred prisoners on board, and they'll all be sick. The Russians only send them home when they're no longer fit to work."

She was worried about the clothes. It wasn't possible to buy them and no one had any to spare. Although not very hopeful, I had a whip-round the mess from the men, managing to drag one pair of woollen socks with holes in the heels, and two shapeless old pullovers; but at least they were wool. And through friends I was able to get hold of an ancient dufflecoat.

Ursula and Hans started life together again in the living space allotted to them by the housing authorities. Hans was in a poor state of health, and his mental outlook had completely changed. Ursula was finding it very difficult, but she struggled on for nearly six months. It was no good and luckily Hans realised it too, but not until he'd found another woman did Ursula leave him and return to Gerhard. However, that situation was not to last much longer. She fell in love with a widowed doctor who had two daughters, married him and became an ordinary Hausfrau; which was what she'd always wanted.

It is not hard to imagine versions of the same little drama being played out countless times in every country where marriages have been roughly torn apart by war.

Now that the Germans were no longer being regarded as the bad boys, friendly relationships, officially encouraged, were gradually building up. A variety of clubs and associations sprouted. The most select was the Anglo-German, a faithful replica of one of the famous old London Clubs. Deep leather armchairs where members could doze behind their newspapers or talk business in lowered tones; subdued lighting; thick carpets; discreet waiters on the alert for a beckoning finger, or other sign of animation.

In contrast the Cosmopoliton Club, with its sociable bar and restaurant, provided a lively meeting-place for all the different nationalities in the city; and at the Frauenklub, women could get together on equal terms to hear talks and discuss mutual problems over a cup of coffee — real coffee now!

As Winston Churchill remarked about the British and Americans during the war, both sides were becoming more 'mixed up'.

H

Part 5

A day to remember, a red letter day, a milestone — call it what you like, it was all of those — the day of the Currency Reform. The three western allies had grown tired of waiting for the Russians to co-operate. So here it was. On 20th July 1948, the old Reichmark was dead and gone, and all accounts blocked. Every German resident in the British, French and American zone was alotted forty new Deutschmarks. All day people waited in long winding queues to collect the new money. It was said that on that day, a tram conductor with nineteen children, was the richest man in West Germany. The first big step on the road to recovery, leading to what subsequently became known as the economic miracle — 'die Wirtschaftswunder' — had been taken.

Under the direction of Professor Erhard, the financial wizard, the laws of supply and demand began to operate freely and things really started to move. Overnight, shop windows which up till now had displayed only worthless knick-knacks and empty cartons, suddenly bulged with all the treasures of Aladdin's cave — only that these treasures were even more desirable, food, ordinary household articles, clothes, furniture, goods that had not been seen for years. Crowds of people stood gazing in the shop windows, absolutely dumbfounded, like children spellbound by the transformation scene in a pantomime. I was amazed to see in a grocer's, not far from the mess, whole plucked geese, eggs, slabs of butter and cheese.

Displayed in another shop were china cups and saucers, plates, pots and pans and cutlery. I even spotted a new sewing-machine. After years of bartering, scrounging and scavenging normal shopping was about to be resumed.

Perhaps most welcome of all, was the return of the sausage. To us, let's face it, a sausage is nothing more than a banger to eke out a plateful of potato mash, fried onions and bacon and egg; but to the Germans it is a theme for endless variations. Entire shops are devoted to its glorification.

The first time I stood in front of one of these shops, I was overcome with awe and wonder at the wealth of imagination and ingenuity that had gone into the devising of the myriad curved shapes there paraded; fat sausages and thin sausages, criss-crossed in enormous piles, or lying in coiled masses; ring-shaped sausages, suitable for use as deck quoits; horseshoe sausages; sausages looped into nooses; hefty sausages in snug white vests, hanging from hooks like the pendulums of grandfather clocks; and reclining sausages split open to lay bare their interiors, each identified by a neatly printed label — Mettwurst, Hackwurst, Leberwurst, Blutwurst, Bratwurst, Kochwurst. From this lot I picked a Kochwurst. It looked to be as packed full of goodies as a Christmas stocking. Having failed to understand the significance of its prefix, I set about frying it in the normal way. Frantic sizzling was followed by a small bang as the wurst blasted off into orbit, and no wonder, it was meant for boiling. Bratwurst is for frying.

How many kinds of wurst are there, I asked a German friend? He laughed and said he'd never counted them. He guessed about thirty, or more. Just think of it, all those variations on the humble basic sausage, and this in a country where individuality and deviation from a standard pattern has for long been discouraged!

To a simple mind it was inexplicable how such an elementary and direct measure as the currency reform could change, almost at a stroke, the whole business of buying and selling, setting the country off on the road to ecomonic recovery and ultimate prosperity. All this time, goods and foodstuffs had been held back by those unconcerned with the welfare of their fellow countrymen. Hard to avoid asking — did it have to happen? Had the currency reform been implemented earlier, there is little doubt that much hardship could have been averted, but governments 'move in a mysterious way, their blunders to perform'.

Now other countries looked on in astonishment at the speed of reconstruction and return to civilised normality. Often on leave in England I would be asked, "How do they do it?" and then, "But of course the Germans work much harder than we do," — forgetting the financial help given soon after the war by the Marshall Aid Plan; and the aid that we could ill afford to send. All that, combined with the new economic measures and working around the clock, plus the vital ingredient of will-power, produced the 'miracle'.

But it wasn't to be all plain sailing. A nasty black cloud already darkened the blue horizon. I was in England when news came through of the Russian blockade of West Berlin, cutting off all supplies. As always on the return journey I felt weighed down by depression and homesickness; this time it was worse. I dreaded going back in the middle of all the sabre-rattling. On the boat-train to Harwich, I actually heard two men discussing the possibility of war with Russia. Hamburg was uncomfortably close to the Russian zone across the Baltic. We had an officers' leave centre at Travemünde, a popular Baltic seaside resort. On the sands an old man with an even older telescope used to invite us on payment of ten pfennigs to have a look at the Russians, as if they were a rare species of jungle animal, but all we ever saw was sand.

In Hamburg the atmosphere was electric with tension and war talk. If the Russians wanted to invade they could just start the tanks rolling across the border. There were two occasions when I kept a small bag packed, ready to leave at a moment's notice. That was one of them and the other the Suez crisis. Should a war break out there is no place like home.

Then began that audacious and imaginative venture, the Berlin airlift, with fleets of planes flying over the country day and night to keep the west of the divided city supplied with food and other essentials; even loads of coal were brought by air. We liked to visit a spot on the river Elbe to watch the huge white Sunderland flying boats descend, skimming smoothly to a halt on the water. You almost felt they should rear up and flap their wings like sea-birds, satisfied with a good touchdown. Ferry boats went out to meet the Sunderlands, and within twenty minutes the planes were fully loaded and off again to Berlin.

When, the following April, the blockade was lifted, West Germany was gravitating towards the allies. In the CCG, the dreaded word 'redundant' had already begun to lift its ugly head. Once again the totally unexpected was happening. On recruitment some higher ranks had been told that possibly we would occupy Germany for at least twenty years. I could see the writing on the wall. Hamburg Radio had received its charter to operate as an independent broadcasting station, remodelled on the pattern of the BBC. It had become Norddeutscher Rundfunk, the North German Radio, under a German director; but because there appeared to be nobody else to do my job, it was agreed that for the time being I should carry on.

Franz took me aside, "Tell me as soon as you get your redundancy notice," he said, "and don't worry. We want you to stay on and continue to work for us."

Just before Christmas, I received an extremely friendly letter from the CCG Director of Education, saying they were regrettably obliged to take me redundant because in effect the CCG was subsidising Hamburg Radio, which, now being under German management, should be paying me for the work. Hard on the heels of this appreciative letter came the official notice from the Foreign Office, beginning grandly . . . .
'Madam,

I am directed by the Secretary of State for Foreign Affairs to give you a month's formal notice that your engagement in the Control Commission for Germany will terminate on 25th December 1949.'

The letter then went on to say that efforts would be made to find me a suitable post in the Public Service under the Crown. Finally a reminder that the Official Secrets Act still applied, even after the engagement had been terminated.

With enormous satisfaction I replied that I had no desire to take up an appointment under the Crown, because the Germans had requested me to stay on doing the same job.

Franz, now head of the Schools' Broadcasting Department, told me that they were prepared to offer me a contract at DM one thousand per month. If I took up the offer he would of course be my boss and the tables would be neatly turned. That after three and a half years in the occupation, I should have crossed over to work for the 'other side' would, on arrival as a low-life recruit, have appeared to me beyond the bounds of fantasy and, judging by the confused reaction of the British and German authorities, such an unlikely happening had not been envisaged, and no contingency plans existed.

Acceptance of the offer meant 'going on the German economy', renouncing all the facilities to which members of the occupation forces were entitled; but with my DM salary, Franz said I could live quite well, although it was still not possible to change the DM into sterling.

The next move was to get permission from some 'higher authority' because technically we were still in a state of war with Germany. The peace treaty had not yet been signed. Once I'd left the CCG and the magic words 'Government Official' had been deleted from my passport, and my Military Entry Permit cancelled, I was at a loose end in the country, a kind of displaced person. I discovered, however, that in the meantime I could remain for a short period as a 'visitor'. Until things got sorted out it seemed the best thing to do. But the full realisation that I was alone and out in the cold swept over me when I saw stamped in my passport in three languages the bleak words . . .

No facilities

Pas de facilité

Keine facilitäten

Now I had to climb on to the bureaucratic merry-go-round, but sadly there was nothing merry about this particular one. First stop, the German labour exchange, accompanied by a kind producer from the radio station. My only other experience of a labour exchange, or employment office, had been in Southampton during the war, and I decided then and there it would be my last. However, that place was the height of old world elegance and courtesy compared with the German variety. A large delapidated ugly building surrounded by cleared bomb sites, it was packed to the walls with shabby hopeless-looking people; mostly refugees from the Russian occupied eastern areas. They sat huddled and silent in rows along benches and on the floors of corridors and passageways. We took our place among them. There could of course be no special treatment for me now. I was applying for permits to live and work in Hamburg just as they were.

After three hours of miserable waiting I was admitted to the inner shrine and informed that I could not be given a permit to work until I'd had permission from the British authorities to stay. I explained that I'd been told by the British that they couldn't give me permission to stay until they'd seen my employment permit from the German office. So it was back on the old roundabout only to discover that no permits of any sort would be granted until I had found accommodation. The frustration was beginning to erode my spirit and will to go on. Why not give up the whole idea and board the next train and ship for UK? No, why let 'them' defeat me? I'd just stay put. Week after week the machinery went creaking on bit by bit till finally the moment of victory. It was like receiving, after years of hard study, your degree or diploma. I was presented with the document coveted by thousands of refugees — my Aufenthaltsbescheinigung — another monster for Mark Twain's collection! It permitted me to live for one year in Hamburg. After that it would have to be renewed regularly. So much in demand was this bit of paper, that a thriving business in forgery existed; the black market price being one thousand marks each. For this reason I was not allowed to have a copy. It soon became clear that my 'defection' to the other side had by no means yet been sanctioned. The military government seemed at a loss how to deal with this curious case. Apparently there had to be a tripartite agreement, involving the French and American authorities, to allow me to work for the Germans. The whole thing seemed to me to be blown up out of all proportion. What on earth did they think I was plotting? Was I another Mata Hari planning a career in espionage, but whom would I be spying on? I had been informed in confidence by a CCG acquaintance that I had even been vetted by the British Intelligence Branch — real cloak and dagger stuff. A pity there was nothing in it!

I'd left the mess in February to stay with friends, and it was now March. Luckily, owing to some clerical oversight for which I was extremely grateful, I'd been receiving my CCG pay as well as my new salary in German marks. The search for permanent accommodation soon had to begin in earnest. I had given up all hope of being allocated official 'living space', and German colleagues advised me to look for a room to rent in a private house. Shortly after starting this exercise, a deep depression enveloped me like a grey army blanket. Having studied the advertisements for rooms to let I selected a house in quite a pleasant area. Outside it looked in reasonably good order, but inside the scene resembled the work of a smash and grab gang. I had to pick my way through hundreds of fragments and chunks of tiles and metal scattered all over the floor of the entrance hall.

"That was our boiler," the landlady informed me, "it exploded. You can have the room if first you pay 200 marks for it to be repaired."

She really had a nerve. I wondered whether she would ever get some homeless wretch to pay for the repair of her rotten old boiler. It didn't look as if it could possibly be put together again.

My next port of call was a large derelict apartment house. Before showing me the room the landlady insisted I should see the bathroom.

"We're very lucky to have a bathroom in the house," she observed, opening the door.

The bath was one of those things known as a 'Sitzbad', a small uncomfortable receptacle with a sort of raised shelf where you park your backside with legs hunched up in front. Stuck in little holders around all four walls were rows and rows of tooth-brushes. There must have been forty or more. I'd seen enough, and told the landlady I had no wish to look at the room, whereupon she launched into a torrent of German which sounded ruder than it probably was.

After this I thought I might strike lucky. I knocked on the door of a solid, respectable-looking house not far from the radio station. With much clanking of keys the door was opened by a genuine teutonic type, a sort of Brunhilde, with statuesque figure and straight yellow hair scraped back into a large bun. A black velvet ribbon encircled her neck. Further down I stared hypnotised by the rhythm of the outsized cameo brooch rising and falling with the ups and downs of her pillowy bosom. She was swathed from head to foot in glistening black. No sooner had I set foot inside the house than the place was rent by wild screams.

"Gott in Himmel! What is the matter?" I said in my best German.

"It's only the maid," she replied. "She's having hysterics again. We've sent for the police."

My first thought was to put as much space as possible between that ill-omened house and myself, but the police car had already arrived and it occurred to me that if they saw a rapidly disappearing figure they might give chase. Screaming with fright the helpless girl was bundled into the car and driven off at speed. Where to? I wondered, and why? Was it a crime to indulge in hysterics? I thought if I stayed much longer I would be on the verge of hysteria myself, and the police would return for me.

Brunhilde led the way upstairs to the room, and instantly my heart went into one of its now familiar nose-dives. The room had a musty smell with long strips of mud-coloured wallpaper hanging down, revealing the plaster behind pitted with holes. There was an ancient rickety bed, and no other furniture except a single hard chair; and on the bare floor, a frayed grubby little rug. Nevertheless, growing desperate, I agreed to take this undesirable living-space at a rent of 100 marks a week, which she demanded in advance.

At seven in the evening all the lights in the house were switched off. Wandering about upstairs I would discern sinister shadows moving silently in and out of doors. The atmosphere gave me the creeps. One of the shadows gradually assumed the form of a bent old woman. Padding up to me and pointing a thumb downwards she croaked, "The people here not nice," before disappearing into the darkness.

The one rusty old bath was kept filled with sticks of firewood and lumps of coal. For washing there was only cold water. If you wanted hot water you had to pay for the heating, which from all accounts involved a technical process as complex as setting up a nuclear reactor. I decided it was all too much and I would beg a bath from friends.

The house was managed by Brunhilde and her mother, a formidable hag, also encased like a beetle in glossy black armour. They had a private room downstairs, and whenever I came in late I could see a slit of light where the door was always kept slightly ajar. I felt convinced they were spying on me, monitoring all my movements.

One afternoon, having a query, I knocked on the door. They

were all there sitting stiffly at a long table; Brunhilde, her mother, the aged gardener and the little maid, who had evidently made a come-back.

"Ach, Frau Melrose," said Brunhilde. "Willkommen to join our little meeting. We have the meeting each Friday. You see, we are working for the return of an emperor for Germany. We think that would be best for our beloved Fatherland — a new Bismark!"

After a week, feeling my tenuous hold on reality fast slipping away, I packed my bag and left. Some English friends, the Blakes, with whom I took refuge, offered me a spare room in their house, which was somewhat irregular — I being no longer entitled to accommodation in requisitioned property.

Most British families had larger houses than they needed, often with several spare rooms. An army sergeant called regularly on his round of inspection, but on that day I could always make myself scarce. Both parties benefited from the arrangement. I had a comfortable home and my hosts received rent in the new valuable Deutschmarks. We all agreed to keep quiet about the transaction. It was a most satisfactory solution to my accommodation problems, of which I'd had more than enough.

British communities abroad seem more closely knit than in the home country — the tribal instinct? The Blakes accepted me as one of the family.

Diana Blake taught in the British School, and her husband worked in a CCG office. They had a small boy of four, Alexander, who was cared for entirely by a resident elderly German nannie, and the two of them used to conduct all their little conversations in German. When an occasion arose for Diana, whose knowledge of German was extremely limited, to scold Alexander for some misdeed, she would often get stuck for the right words. Then Alexander would march impatiently to the bookcase, take out the German/English dictionary and hand it to her saying, "Kuk mal in hier, Mutti" — "Look in here, Mummy," and if she used the wrong gender for a noun the maddening child promptly corrected her, "Nein, Mutti, not 'Das Löffel, Der Löffel'."

Sadly my stay with the Blakes was short. Before they left for

England they passed me on to friends, another couple, the Cooks, who lived in a suburb of Hamburg in a house with a strange roof shaped at one end like a pyramid and flat at the other end. They had an eight-year-old daughter, Alison. A large brown rabbit, Longears, completed the family. The rabbit had the run of the house which he always treated with respect. However, from time to time he did indulge in a single act of vandalism. Should a flex belonging to the electric fire or vacuum-cleaner be left lying on the floor, sensing no doubt in his rabbitty brain the presence of a deadly snake, he would launch a ferocious attack, biting the flex clean through in half a dozen places.

He and Alison often played on the flat roof. While sitting in the living-room one afternoon, gazing dreamily out of the window at the pelting rain, my view was suddenly obstructed by an elongated brown object with flailing legs hurtling from the sky. Could it be raining rabbits as well as cats and dogs? I rushed out to investigate. The daft old bunny had taken a misdirected hop and sailed through the railing around the roof. He was taken off to the vet, returning with one hind leg in plaster, and soon developed an effective three-legged hop.

I grew fond of them all and was sorry when they had to return to UK. However, again I was passed on to friends. Each time I moved house, Herr Moritz, the office porter, used to load my one suitcase, plus a crate of books and scripts onto his little handcart, and wheel it through the streets of Hamburg. In the office they jokingly decided that to save ink they would henceforth register my address only in pencil, and rub it out with every change.

There were to be many more entries and rubbings-out. It was an unsettled way of living. Each couple or family, within the restrictions of the occupation, had its own life-style, and I had to keep adjusting to the different patterns. I would get drawn too, into arguments and rows, but at least it was never dull, and I was always made to feel at home.

The Haywards employed a young German maid, Renate, who every Saturday morning insisted that we all sit round the kitchen table to do the Toto — the German football pools. None of us knew anything about the matches, teams or league tables. Renate thought I was crazy when, with half-closed eyes and a pin, I made random stabs at the forecasts. But . . . the following week in comes the rheumaticy old postman for his cup of coffee, sits down at the table, opens his satchel, draws out a large purse and hands over thirty marks. I'd got eleven correct results, and of course so had thousands of others. Anyway, we celebrated with a bottle of Steinhager, the fearsome German gin, and sent the old postman reeling on his way.

Although I was now on the German economy, and officially had no facilities, there were a good many advantages. For instance I could go on leave travelling by the Scandinavian Express, a civilized comfortable train running between Copenhagen and the Hook of Holland. Returning from my first leave in this pleasant manner I settled down, from time to time checking that my bulging suitcase was still in its place on the rack. It contained nearly all my personal belongings.

In England for the first time since the war I had been able to afford really good new clothes, including shoes. For years I possessed only two pairs, one for day and one for evening. I had acquired a smart grey flannel suit; 'a little black dress', almost obligatory for cocktail parties; and an elegant two-piece to wear at the wedding of CCG friends, which I was due to attend the next day in Hamburg.

The only other person in the compartment was a dumpy, round-faced German girl who tucked herself up and went to sleep, her head against the window. The three seats opposite, with reservation tabs over them, remained empty. This was obviously disturbing to the orderly minds of the train officials who at regular intervals demanded to know whether they were still free. Presently, a young woman and a girl of about twelve were ushered in. The woman, a slim rather sharp-featured blonde was smartly dressed and not unattractive. She sat down opposite the German girl and addressed a remark to her in English.

"You can speak your own language," replied the girl. "I am German too," and then it started. Lapsing delightedly into her native language, the woman poured out the story of her life. I eavesdropped while pretending to be engrossed in my book. She was living in England, married to an Englishman. "Yes, he was one of those Control Commission types until he went back. He told me he had always wanted a German wife and came to Germany to get one. Then he picked on me. I was a war widow, and had my little girl, Renate, to keep. That was in 1949. We live in Manchester. What a place! You don't need any good clothes, only a raincoat and overshoes; but we have a nice home. Of course you can't live in England unless you both work. My husband's in the police, and I've got a job in the air ministry. What do you call that in German? I'm forgetting my own language — Luftwaffeministerium — yes that's it. Our income is £14 a week, but that's nothing in England. Renate goes to secondary school and must have a uniform. We have to buy it. Cheek, I call it! Soldiers, police and firemen get their uniform free, but you have to pay for the children's. Of course they have this health service. Any visiting foreigner can get free glasses and free false teeth. I think only people who work should get such things free. Now you've been in England, haven't you? Don't you think Englishmen are selfish? In the evenings I want to go out and dance or do something but, no, my husband says, 'Why go out when it's so cosy at home?' and he sits there with his crossword puzzle or football pools until I think I'll go mad. What I miss in England are the little dance places and cafés with a cabaret. There's nothing but those dreadful pubs, always full of men, and they serve the beer slopping over the side of the glass. Imagine that in Germany! And the endless cups of tea. The English live for their tea. The food is terrible, flabby fish and chips, and everything else in tins.''

The two girls burst into fits of laughter as they discussed the topic of English food.

We were now in Germany, and as she gazed out of the window, the blonde went into rhapsodies over the homeland. ''Oh, to be back in Germany for three whole months!'' But she was in such a dilemma. Should she return to Germany for ever? The situation was complicated, it would mean a divorce and that would cost money. Then there was the nationality difficulty now that she had a wretched British passport.

The conversation, or rather monologue, continued until we reached Bremen where the younger girl, with an ''Auf Wiedersehen'' got out.

I wondered what she would decide, and how many other German girls who, in the expectation of a better life had been eager to marry Englishmen, were soon to become like her, homesick and disillusioned. Instead of a land grown rich and comfortable, luxuriating in the spoils of victory, they had found a country enfeebled by the long struggle, with some war-time regulations such as the rationing of basic foodstuffs still in force. One heard stories, too, of how the German brides were not always made welcome by the husband's family and friends.

Towards the end of the journey I fell asleep and missed the main railway station, not waking up till we reached Altona, the next station on the line, where there seemed to be a great deal of activity — police and the army milling around. I rang up an army friend to ask if he could send transport for me. After about half an hour, a fifteen-hundredweight truck arrived. The driver threw my suitcase into the back, and I got in front beside him. We had travelled only about a quarter of a mile before another British army vehicle overtook us and stopped in the middle of the road blocking our way.

"Did you know you had a man in the back of your truck?" shouted the driver, running towards us.

My driver and I both sprang out and rushed to the back of the truck. He shone his torch all round inside but there was nothing there.

"The bastard, he's got away with it," he said. "We'll never catch him."

The whole area, mostly ruins, was in complete darkness. We went back to the station and informed the police, but got no satisfaction from either the British or Germans. They didn't want to know. "It happens every day; there's nothing we can do about it. Besides, we're awaiting the arrival of the King of Sweden."

Blow the King of Sweden! I felt absolutely desolate, stripped, bereft. Suddenly I had nothing — no pyjamas, tooth-brush, washing things. My treasured photographs and letters gone forever, and no smart clothes for the wedding, or for that matter, any other social event.

At my old mess, friends rallied round and lent me all that was necessary. I'd often had to listen to other people constantly complaining that they'd had their possessions stolen — bottles of spirits, cigarettes, clothes — but I'd been in the habit of boasting that I'd never lost a thing, which was true; and now in one instant I had lost practically all my worldly goods. The lesson: it *can* happen to you!

Fears that my social life in the CCG would come to an end once I was 'on the German economy' proved unjustified. Although the CCG was gradually being run down I still had plenty of friends. Parties were as numerous as ever, some falling into new categories, redundancy parties, farewell parties, pregnancies, engagements — any old pretext would do.

'There's nowt so queer as folk', and certainly the CCG had its share of unconventional and often odd characters; men and women whose personalities were of such an outstanding and dominant nature, they had the effect wherever they appeared of reducing all others present to the sameness of peas in a pod. Franz was such a person and Nigel another.

During the war, Nigel had served as a lieutenant in the Royal Navy, but always called himself Commander. When I got to know him he told me the truth and asked me to keep up the pretence. He said it gave him more prestige, and didn't he look every inch a commander? I had to admit he did. Over six feet tall and broad with it, he was preposterously vain. On arriving for a date his first remark, without fail, "How do I look?" And he would strut around preening himself. "How do you like my new suit? What do you think of this tie?" and then invariably, "Nice day for the race."

"What race?"

"The human race!"

At parties he would revel in the limelight, telling joke after joke, all crude schoolboyish stuff, finally insisting on rendering each story into German. Bad enough in English but in his German even cruder and ruder! He worked in a low grade as a CCG clerk, but having a rich father who provided him with a regular allowance, he had no ambition, being perfectly content with his job, which demanded no 'brainwork'. He was crazy about ships, and every Sunday morning insisted we go on a Hafenrundfahrt — good word that — a trip around the harbour which took nearly three hours. Now that the port was slowly returning to normal it was always fascinating to watch ships from all over the world entering and leaving through the long Elbe estuary. With demolition at an end, work in the dry docks and the world famous shipyards was being resumed, but some of the enormous damage could still be seen. All that remained of the huge U-boat pens built of concrete, metres thick, and heavily camouflaged, were tumbled heaps of blocks strewn around like children's toy bricks.

"Talking to people is my hobby," Nigel was fond of saying. Wherever he found himself, in a train, tram, ship, café, or outside walking, he lost no time in starting up a conversation in his fluent, though excruciating German. Not as you might expect, about himself, or choosing only attractive girls, but with every man, woman or child. He didn't give a damn however unprepossessing or poor and shabby the people. Opening up with one of his truly awful jokes, within a few minutes he had them laughing, and confiding in him. If it were the custom for a person to introduce himself with a signature tune, Nigel's, would certainly have been, 'Spread a little happiness as you go by.'

I soon discovered, however, a less appealing facet of his character: he was a scrounger, forever cadging cigarettes and drinks, although both were cheap and plentiful. And he had no scruples about 'borrowing' my precious Deutschmarks.

In due course he went the way of all CCG flesh, back to the rigours of post-war life in UK. Whether Nigel contributed anything to the cause of re-education, rehabilitation or democratization — those high sounding concepts laid down in official policy documents — is a debatable point; but one suspects that with his jovial good humour and uninhibited friendliness towards the German people he added more to the gaiety of nations than did many worthy characters in top administration. For every flamboyant character like Nigel there were many people who expressed their sympathy with the German community in quieter more modest fashion.

One charming warm-hearted lady, wife of a prominent official, was rarely to be found seated without her knitting, needles clicking away at great speed.

On enquiring what she was making she would hold up a narrow white strip and tell you.

"It's going to be a warm petticoat for a poor old lady I've heard of. Isn't it terrible, she has no proper underclothes," or "It's a vest for a poor little baby." But no matter how she described the article, it always looked much the same at every stage, a tube-like stocking. A recurrent image used to pass before my eyes — a dachshund on a cold winter's day trotting along warmly encased in one of these garments.

Another CCG wife acted towards the Germans like a dutiful Edwardian lady distributing largesse among the parishioners. She busied herself collecting small unwanted things, declaring "Someone will find a use for them." And whenever she heard from her domestic staff of a sick person in the family, she at once set off for the house bearing little gifts and a flask of hot soup.

While in Britain food rationing was still in operation — it didn't end until 1954 — I found myself in the unbelievable position of being able to buy food freely on the German market for dispatch to Britain. At regular intervals I used to send parcels of sugar, butter, tins of ham and other meats to my family, with the thought, what an extraordinary irony, food from the recently defeated country to the victorious one! But it seemed that in the fast changing pattern of events, irony and the unexpected, formed the only constant threads.

My new reversed relationship with Franz, he now the boss and I the underling, was going smoothly with no significant change in attitudes, although I thought I detected a slightly different manner adopted towards me by some of the other staff. A sort of 'You're one of us now', mingled with a certain amount of suspicion and very occasionally hostility; or it could have been resentment at my presence on the staff; understandable at the time.

Work was expanding in various directions. The terms of my contract stipulated that in edition to writing the scripts, I had to do anything else that I was asked to undertake, without extra payment. I did translations, still had my visits to schools and discussions with teachers at conferences and gave cheery little radio talks clarifying, I hoped, the dark mysteries of typical British institutions like public schools and cricket. I can assure anyone attempting to interpret the rules of cricket to a foreign audience, in a foreign language, will be in for a run of sleepless nights. For a start how do you explain the term 'maiden over'? 'The mind boggles!' as they say, and the story of the ashes sounds pretty daft to German ears. With all the extra work went a slight feeling of strain. Although now it seems unreasonable, in those days of the occupation, a British person certainly was regarded by the native population as a representative of his country and I, being the only one working for the North German Radio, couldn't help feeling very conscious of this.

Becoming more prosperous every day, Franz took a perverse delight at social gatherings, and even conferences, in telling stories about the early days of the CCG. Over and over again he would relate how he used to bring his scripts to the office for me to vet, and after a cursory glance I would OK them with my initials; and the time I took to smoking with a holder, and he complained to me that the cigarette ends he collected from the ashtrays were too short. Watching the expressions, I had the feeling that many of the listeners did not share his amusement, preferring to put those memories of humiliation and hardship behind them.

Word soon got round the British community that I was 'useful to know', the idea being that I could help people to earn Deutschmarks in broadcasting either by acting or writing. I would get telephone calls from visitors recently arrived in the country, and most days someone called wanting to see me. So it was all in the day's work when a clerk told me that an Englishman was waiting in reception with a letter of introduction. A huge broad tough chap, he reminded me of Nigel, except for the face which struck me as being rather unpleasant. He didn't smile and his eyes, close set and narrow, were of the kind often described as shifty. Without speaking he handed me the letter, which was from a friend of mine, the Director of the British Forces Network Radio Station, saying that the bearer, Mr Donald Milner, had been to see him about a job, and he'd suggested to him that he should have a talk with me about the possibility of suitable work in German radio, adding that Mr Milner spoke good German.

After I'd put a few questions to him, he cut me short, saying, "It's so hot in here. Why don't we go and have a beer outside at the café on the corner?" A suggestion to which I readily agreed.

Over our beer I tried to find out something about him, and what he actually wanted. He'd been in the CCG, but left after about a year, he told me. That I thought was odd because there were few people who voluntarily left the CCG. He said it was to start an export business for which he needed more money.

"Have you had any exciting experiences or adventures that you could write a script about?" I asked, continuing my interrogation.

Giving me what can only be described as 'a funny look' he murmured, "Oh, nothing special."

I suggested he should try to write a script, send it in and I would do what I could to help. He invited me out to lunch but as usual I obeyed my intuition, making some excuse.

It was several months later while in a friend's house that I picked up a page of a British newspaper and there staring out at me was the unpleasant face of Donald Milner . . . . .

THE MAN INTERPOL ARE SEEKING
IN CONNECTION WITH THE MURDER OF
HIS WIFE AND MOTHER-IN-LAW

Not long afterwards in a wood near Cologne, with the net tightening around him, Donald Merrett, alias Donald Milner, alias Ronald Chesney, alias Leslie Chown, put an end to his script with a bullet through the head.

A book, *Chesney, the Fabulous Murderer*, told the story of his life of crime from the day when as a young man in Edinburgh he faced trial on a charge of murdering his mother — the verdict, unproven. On leaving home to 'earn' his living he had adopted a string of aliases. As a war-time naval officer in command of a ship, his gallantry had been acknowledged by the Admiralty. Then in the unstable climate of post-war Europe, he quickly discovered that easy pickings were to be made from smuggling, and took it up as a profession, dealing with every kind of scarce commodity from diamonds to dope: a blackmailer, car thief, gun-runner, swindler, parasite, he stopped at nothing, and by means of bribery and corruption of customs' officials bluffed his way through Europe, seeing on his travels the inside of almost every jail on the continent and in North Africa. And this was the man I had interviewed, enquiring if he'd had any exciting experiences he could write about!

By now I had tackled almost everything in broadcasting, but hadn't given a thought to television. I usually had my lunch in the radio canteen, because it was less boring than eating alone, and a good place to make contacts; it was there that Herr Schröder-Jahn, a TV producer, approached me.

"Frau Melrose, what would you think about taking part in a television play?" Observing my blank reaction, he continued, "I am looking for someone to play the part of a nineteenth century English governess who speaks German with an English accent."

Well, that would be no problem! I hadn't yet refused a challenge, and so once again rashly agreed to attempt something I knew absolutely nothing about, and was probably quite incapable of doing.

"I haven't done much acting," I said, "and none in TV."

"That doesn't matter. It's an important part but not very long, and I shall be your producer."

The play, based on a sensational case in nineteenth century France, centred on a court-martial. My role was that of Miss Allen, an English governess to an aristocratic young lady. Most of the part was taken up with giving evidence against the young French officer accused of entering her room at night. Whether anything worse happened was not made clear. With the exception of myself the cast consisted of professional actors, a tricky situation for me. Determined not to let the side down, I conscientiously learnt all my lines in time for the first reading, which evoked cries of admiration; it being 'Not done' to learn one's lines so early in rehearsal.

The studios were in one of the giant concrete bunkers, where, during the thousand bomber raids on Hamburg known as 'die Katastrophe', hundreds of people had spent days and nights of terror while the bombs fell and the fires raged. According to official statistics, more buildings were destroyed in those raids than in the whole of the United Kingdom during the war. There was no street fighting in Hamburg, the damage being done by air attacks alone.

Inside the bunker it was horribly bare, damp and dispiriting; the atmosphere still exuding the smell of fear; a place hardly conducive to settling down in a world of make-believe. Rehearsals went on every day for three weeks, during which time, with Herr Schröder-Jahn playing Swengali to my Trilby, I could feel myself growing into the character of Miss Allen;

timid, narrow, prudish. The clothes specially made for me, were extremely uncomfortable. The dress of a coarse green material, had a long skirt, tight waist, high collar and 'mutton-leg' sleeves. On the set my dresser trailed after me bearing a decrepit fur stole and gold-rimmed pince-nez on a little tray to hand over at the right moment and, to lend authenticity to my new career I had my own dressing-room, the name on the door, nicely misspelt — Mrs Georgi*nana* Melrose.

The intense heat generated by the profusion of lamps everywhere, hanging from the roof, along the walls and on the floor, combined with the absence of fresh air and daylight, brought on attacks of claustrophobia, especially during the long periods of waiting. While actually speaking my lines I had absolutely no feelings of my own because I had become a different person; I just felt myself to be that elderly, straight-laced spinster, Miss Allen; but sometimes small things were likely to disturb the illusion. From time to time, even when I was engaged in a dialogue, a cameraman would march up and adjust my head to the required angle, as one might twist the head of a wooden puppet, and I was expected to continue as if I hadn't noticed. However, something that really shattered my concentration happened while I was giving evidence in my big scene. With the camera on me for close-up, I sat at a table facing the 'colonel' in full dress uniform, his round bald head shining like a polished cricket ball when, in the middle of an emotional speech, describing how at midnight I had witnessed the young officer entering the room of my charge through the window, a lady appeared from nowhere and began tenderly to dab his glowing pate with a jumbo-sized swansdown powder-puff, for all the world as if dusting off a baby's bottom. Proceedings held up due to collapse of Miss Allen in damp heap of giggles!

Herr Schröder-Jahn directed my every movement, demonstrating all the gestures to be performed. In fact, when in the mood he would play every role in turn, including that of the girl dancing for joy in her boudoir, an absurdly comic sight, the big silver-haired man, normally so grave, pirouetting and doing gazelle leaps around the set, then sitting down in front of the mirror to 'put his hair up'.

The 'colonel', with whom I had most of my scenes, never

stayed on the set unless he was in a scene actually being shot, but disappeared into the canteen to refuel with his favourite schnapps, returning only on call and then more often than not giving me the wrong cue, which for someone new to the game was disconcerting to say the least; in fact, the whole business was stressful. I suppose most film producers have to be hard task-masters. Herr Schröder-Jahn would not tolerate slackness from any member of the cast or film crew, neither would he accept excuses. He put his hands on my shoulders.

"Frau Melrose, you have no business to be tired," he said, earnestly, after I'd explained that my poor showing was due to a late night, "we have bought you body and soul."

One thousand marks was the price they'd paid for my dubious services to television.

Although the play was being recorded, the final performance, beamed to West Germany and Austria, was to go out 'live', a fact mercifully concealed from me till the last moment. While waiting for the countdown the actors wandered around restlessly, telling each other to stretch an arm out in front, in order to watch for signs of nerves. Most of the hands were shaking a bit, but none as much as mine. In another little tribal ritual, a person would silently approach you from behind and putting his mouth over your ear, bellow down it, "Toi . . toi . . toi!" which I gathered meant something like good luck. Then it was stand-by for the countdown . . . "eins . . zwei . . drei . . vier . . . fünf . . . we had lift-off! And at that moment I couldn't imagine that shooting through space could hold more terrors than being 'on the air' down below.

At the end, I think we all felt that we had put that little extra into our performances, a heightened sensibility, but what were the thoughts of the boss? We awaited the verdict — thumbs up! Then on a wave of euphoria we were borne along in the direction of the canteen with only one thought in mind, a drink. On his corner table the 'colonel's' schnapps awaited its consumer. Now his bald dome, recently guilty of reflecting unwanted and confusing lights, had been allowed to return to its natural state, glistening with dewdrops.

Humbling to think that all our efforts over the past three weeks amounted to no more than a trifle, for millions of people an hour or so of distraction, forgotten by this time next week, or sooner, but that's 'show biz'.

Once I had cast off the worn-out skin of Miss Allen, I felt as gratified as a snake must feel after completing that laborious operation, and if the skin underneath didn't seem all that fresh, at least it was my own.

"Now, how would you like to become an actress?" the others wanted to know, and such was their fervent belief that of all professions acting rated the noblest, there were gasps of disbelief when I said firmly, "Decidedly no!"

For me the most satisfying part of the whole experience came next day with the 'spin-off', going into shops, people turning to stare, and being greeted in tones of respect and admiration by those I knew, "Oh, Frau Melrose, we saw you on television last night. Prima!" — very morale boosting — all is vanity. My incursion into the acting profession left me with the conviction that my team, at any rate, would never find itself promoted to the first division of the modesty league.

It was during the fifties that one really became aware of the accelerating speed of reconstruction, no more despairing talk of needing twenty years simply to clear the ruins. Work went on all day and by floodlight through the night, and the task wasn't left only to the workmen and labourers; almost every able-bodied man and woman at some time became a 'workman', not scorning to use hands in hard physical labour. Acrimonious arguments over wages, hours of work, pay demands, differentials, percentages, etc., were patently irrelevent. Most people seemed to regard it as a privilege to be playing a part in the rebuilding of the city. Once in the office when complaining of having too much work, I met with a rebuke by an elderly professor, "But we are the lucky ones," he said. "We should be thankful that we are able to work."

Day by day the scene changed. Walking along on my way to the office or somewhere, I would stop suddenly noticing that a familiar small oasis on the edge of a bomb site, maybe a little shack selling hot frankfurters, had vanished overnight, leaving a flat, tidy rectangle or a hastily constructed tobacconist-newsagents would have subsided into a rubbish heap. The burnt out shells of buildings awaiting demolition and unable to stand up to the fierce Hamburg gales presented a daily hazard. My nearest miss came when sauntering along a narrow side street I heard behind me a tremendous crash and rumble; a high free-standing wall had toppled, spilling its bricks all over the road seconds after I had passed.

Apathy and discontent had now given way to a feeling of urgency and satisfaction in accepting the tremendous challenge, a sense of relief to be able at last, after years concentrated on the business of destruction, to recreate a new and perhaps even finer Hamburg. But there was an advantage in starting from scratch; it was possible to make use of all the latest technical innovations in science and industry. The new studios in the radio station were fitted with the most modern broadcasting equipment. Magnetaphone tape, with all its potentiality, was in general use for recording, while most other European radio stations were still entirely dependent on records. In those days the tape was quite a novelty and we often had some fun with it in the studio. Should one of the speakers fluff his lines the assistant on the tape machine could cut them out and I would present the actor with a handful of coiled tape resembling a ball of wool after the cat has got at it, and tell him, "Here's your mistake!" It's common knowledge that the nature of tape makes it easy to practise convenient deceptions. After hearing a play-back of a programme of English folk songs, we were not satisfied with John, our English amateur singer, and had him cut out, substituting the voice of a more professional singer. Soon after the programme had been broadcast I ran into John, "Did you hear the song broadcast," I asked him.

"Oh yes," he said.

"And what did you think of your voice?"

"It was much better than I expected, I sounded quite professional," he replied.

Thinking it only fair, I told him tactfully about the mean little trick. Although somewhat taken aback, he reacted with surprising good humour.

'Where there is no vision the people perish'.

Immediately after the war the prospect of rebuilding had seemed an impossible dream. Not only the city but its pride and joy, the port, had been reduced to a graveyard; the wrecks of thousands of ships blocking the Elbe and harbour basin; granaries and warehouses burnt out; docks, slipways and cranes no more than piles of scrap. But there *had* been a vision, and now it was being realised. A few years later the huge port was operating once again, the shipyards busy with repairs and new orders. Ten years after the surrender, the ruins in the city had been cleared or levelled. And more than half the buildings destroyed had been replaced. There was a report in the papers that a party of American journalists from the mid-west arrived to describe and photograph the 'spectacular ruins' but stayed instead to write stories of a spectacular new city springing up.

Walking home at night after an evening out could be a weird experience, the 'Trümmerwagen', the 'ruins train', chugging along the makeshift tracks with its truck loads of rubble; men and women working, often only with shovels, silhouetted in the floodlights against a backdrop of blackened brick walls and dark mountains of debris.

One night Ursula and I, feeling in high spirits, jumped onto the end truck of the 'Trümmerwagen' and had an eerie ride all the way to the dumping place, where we wandered around like souls in hell, completely lost in the sinister, evil-smelling wasteland, and had to be directed home by grinning workmen.

All over the city blocks of offices, flats, schools, churches and factories were shooting up. With few exceptions there appeared to be no attempt to recreate old styles. The new designs were simple, modern, uncluttered. In the suburbs the blocks of flats, well-spaced and solidly built, were of reasonable height, often not more than three or four storeys, with wide balconies, soon to become filled with tubs of flowers and climbing plants. Inevitably the bleak, barrack-type blocks sprouted here and there. It was in one of these that I now had my own home.

Over the years friends and acquaintances had been fading out of my life, shipped unwillingly back to a duller and certainly more sober life in Britain. That callous thing 'redundancy' had been thorough in its work. From time to time the authorities decided that the hurtful 'redundant' with its connotation of being unwanted should be dropped and, presumably after weeks of thought and deliberation behind locked doors, came up with 'Surplus to requirements'.

With the granting in 1955 of full sovereignty for West

Germany, the CCG itself became what many ill-informed people back home had all along declared it to be — 'Surplus to requirements'. Then, having no one anymore on whom to park, I had been forced to look for a place of my own. My flat in one of the large new blocks of yellow brick was financed by a non-profit making workers' co-operative called New Home. The company, conscious of the great number of people left alone after the war, made the sensible decision to build whole blocks expressly for those obliged, or wishing to live on their own. Each flat, designed rather like a ship's cabin, comprised one small room, the bed in a recess, in front of which a curtain could be drawn, a kitchen of cubby-hole dimensions, but complete with mini refrigerator under mini electric stove, and mini sink with a mini water heater. Unfortunately, no window, not even a mini; and a bathroom just spacious enough to allow you to stand and rub a towel across your back. No frills but absolutely adequate for one person.

I have often wondered why, if West Germany with housing problems far more acute than those in Britain, should have been able to build such blocks, it couldn't have been done in London and other big cities to meet the needs of single people with jobs and money, but nowhere suitable to live.

For the disposal of refuse from the flats there was a novel arrangement, at least new at the time, on each floor an aperture in the wall like a porthole. You just lifted the covering flap, tipped your rubbish in and it went clattering down the chute. I assume it landed somewhere in the bowels of the earth beneath the block, but occasionally things could go wrong. The stuff would mount too high before being taken away and on lifting the flap you might get an unpleasant surprise when a smelly pile of debris regurgitated onto the floor. Once, on hearing a scream, we rushed out of our little cells to see a lady standing hypnotised by a startled rat which had tumbled out together with a mess of tea leaves, cabbage stalks and soggy paper bags.

The planners had given some thought to the postman. Not for him the wearisome climb up six flights of stone steps, or the trudge along the maze of narrow corridors to pop the mail through each front door. On the ground floor fixed to the wall were rows of little green metal boxes, each with the name and number of the flat dweller on a label outside. In the morning you had the thrill of unlocking your box never knowing quite what you would find. Besides letters there were frequently little packets of confectionery, face-creams, a mousetrap portion of cheese, and slices of the latest in black bread; all deposited in hope by local tradespeople. We used to comfort ourselves with the thought that if we fell on hard times we could live off the samples in our letter boxes.

Admittance to the block was controlled by an up-to-date intercom system. Hearing the buzz in your flat you just picked up the receiver and asked "Who is it?" before pressing your buzzer to allow the front door to be opened. Quite often all you heard was garbled nonsense shouted by children having a little fun. Once or twice on lifting the receiver I heard yells of "Heil Hitler!" followed by a burst of drunken laughter.

People living alone have, as a rule, a greater need for visitors than most and, because of the constant stream of callers observed entering and leaving the flats, the block became known in the neighbourhood as "Das Haus der Freude" — "The House of Pleasure" — no comment! But I was happy at last to have visitors, be able to have my own parties, and get on with the job, all in a place of my own. It was good to settle down, watch life improve all round with the people every day growing more prosperous, but of course all the misery did not fade away with the end of the war. I imagine there was hardly anyone left without a cross to bear. The times were especially tragic for the millions of so-called 'surplus' young women for whom there was little chance of ever finding a husband and living a normal married life. At one time rumours persisted that in the German Parliament a proposal had been put forward to make it lawful for a man to have two wives. However, nothing came of this daring suggestion, which was perhaps just as well. Many people saw it creating more problems than it would solve.

On Hamburg radio each day for years, a list of names, ages and descriptions of missing persons was broadcast; men, women, children and even babies who, during and immediately after the war, had disappeared without trace. Anyone having information was asked to write in, and now and again you heard that lost people had turned up. Terrible heart-break must have lain behind these interminable lists of names.

People having to endure the torment of not knowing the fate of a loved relative; but it could be argued that in certain cases to know might have made for greater anguish, and would have put an end even to hope.

With so much on my plate, the script-writing, interviewing people to play the parts, and now the productions, recently handed over to me, I was really a one-man band. Although the whole flat would have fitted easily into the average suburban living-room, I didn't feel like lifting a finger to do even the minimum of housework. I had no trouble in finding a Putzfrau, the descriptive title for a cleaner. Everybody was glad of a job. Frau Olde was a small shapeless woman, somewhere between fifty and sixty. Now and again, through the lanky grey strands of hair, hanging like a bead curtain, you could discern a round vacant face. One of the great army of war-widows; she had seen it all. She had survived the Nazis, the'Katastrophe', the British Military Government, and the Control Commission. When I enquired what had happened to her during the war, she said she had been conscripted to work as a cleaner on the trains taking people to the Belsen concentration camp, but always maintained she knew nothing of what went on there, and I believed her.

She was one of those millions all over the world concerned solely with the day to day business of survival, her life bounded by her own four walls and immediate neighbourhood. Continents, countries, governments, international events, appeared to have no meaning for her. Such people seem to be immune to the torments of imagination and hypersensitivity. Frau Olde reminded me of Mrs Harris, the elderly landlady, with whom I lodged for a short time in Southampton during the war.

On the few occasions when I was not out gallivanting in the evenings, I had to share the small living-room with Mrs Harris and together, she with arms folded and knees well apart we would listen to the war news issuing between the crackles and whistles from her ancient wireless set. No matter how horrendous the news — cities bombed; battleships sunk; countries overrun; planes shot down; Hitler ranting to shouts of 'Sieg Heil', her only comment was always the same, "It's all a lota nonsense," uttered in a faintly supercilious tone. Among friends, this innocuous remark caught on like a catchphrase in a radio comedy. Whether trivial or earnest, every statement would unfailingly be met with the response, "It's all a lota nonsense!"

"It's better now," was Frau Olde's sole comment on the recent past, and for most this was true; it was better, much better. She had her own little flat, television, her pension, and wanted nothing more.

Seven years went by and I was beginning to think perhaps it was time to pack up and leave Hamburg. Now that things were more or less normal again, much of the excitement and challenge had gone. I hadn't many English friends left, and deep down could feel the old homesickness gnawing away inside; and home meant England, but there was the job to think of. The last thing I wanted was to give it all up and start looking for another directly I got back. I talked it over with Franz, who was as usual most understanding and reassuring.

"What are you worried about? You can write anywhere. Even on a desert island you could scratch your scripts with a bit of flint on a slab of rock."

"Hmm, you'd have to give me a big rise to help pay the postage to Hamburg."

"Post pre-paid naturally!"

"Anyway," I said, "I'm not going to a desert island. I'm going to live a dull and respectable life behind the lace curtains of suburbia."

"You think so? Lace curtains don't change anything!"

It was gradually dawning on me that a good many things would change; all the same, I was ready for a freer and easier life with less strain and responsibility. For a start, I wouldn't have to search my mind to remember the correct genders of nouns before daring to join in a conversation. I might even forget how to speak German altogether, in which case the loss of one more poor linguist would be of no consequence.

Franz suggested I should give up my contract and work on a freelance basis. "Naturally we'd have to find some other English person to do the productions. We couldn't pay you to come over just to do those, but you could make regular visits for discussions and conferences. So don't worry. There's no reason why everything shouldn't work out very well, and you'll still be getting all those lovely Deutschmarks. They'll soon be better than your old pounds!''

It certainly seemed a satisfactory arrangement. I had lived in Germany for sixteen years in varied circumstances, and in more houses than I could remember. Friends had proposed that outside each house where I'd lived, a commemorative brass plaque should be affixed; Hamburg would be plastered with them!

Scanning the advertisements for flats in the English papers, I came across an artist's impression of three-storey blocks of flats to be built in Surrey, about twenty miles from London, and only a short distance from the airport, which would be convenient for my trips to Hamburg. The caption read . . . *Why not live graciously in an elegant out-of-town flat?*

Why not indeed? It was time for some elegance. A twenty pound refundable deposit was all that was required to secure one of these desirable apartments, and I promptly sent it off.

Plans for the interior design came back by return — a large living-room almost twice as big as my Hamburg flat; two good-sized bedrooms; attractive kitchen and bathroom with views over surrounding grass and trees. I decided to buy. It would not have been worthwhile to have my few sticks of furniture transported to England, and so I presented them to a young German couple about to set up home; and looked forward to starting everything afresh.

In the fifties and sixties, international policies continued to change with the rapidity of scenes in a fast moving film. The Russian Bear had long ago decided to dance to its own tune, stretching out great paws to grab what it could. Although slogans on hoardings proclaimed 'Unteilbares Deutschland' — 'Indivisible Germany', there was no escaping the fact that ever since the end of the war the country had been rigidly divided into East and West. Families had been split up. If you wanted to visit your grandmother in East Germany you had to hack your way through a dense jungle of bureaucracy, and it was well nigh impossible for her to visit you in the West.

Again the 'unthinkable' was happening — although maybe in the light of twentieth century horrors, nothing should be considered 'unthinkable' — the allies were pressing West Germany to rearm and become a partner in the Western Alliance.

Which of us in the CCG could possibly have foreseen the shape of things to come when, instead of headlines in the British Press such as — DO THE GERMANS NEED OUR FOOD? and GERMANY THE RUBBISH HEAP OF EUROPE. We should be reading reports headed — THE NEW WEALTHY WEST GERMANS, DEUTSCHMARKS, THE HARDEST CURRENCY, DEMOCRACY IS WORKING IN WEST GERMANY, WEST GERMANY TO BECOME A MEMBER OF NATO, and HAMBURG THE RICHEST CITY IN EUROPE.

Back in England and settled down happily in my 'Elegant out-of-town flat', I started work again on the radio scripts. In the meantime the destiny that awaits all radio characters had befallen Henry and Barbara: they had been 'written out'. However, they had considerably left behind a son, Sandy, to carry on spreading abroad the reputation of the work-shy Englishman. In the nicest possible sense Sandy quickly became a big brother to many German children.

After sending the first manuscript off to Hamburg, I came away with a story that rarely fails to get a laugh. Having scrutinized the large brown envelope, the post office clerk handed me a form to fill in for the customs — description of goods, value etc. I wrote 'Manuscripts' and left the space for 'value' blank.

"You haven't stated the value of the contents," the clerk told me.

"I don't know," I replied. "They're manuscripts, the value of my brains."

"Oh well," he said briskly, "I'll just write 'no value'."

Naturally to him all my hard work was only another postal packet, but his remark set off a train of thought. I suppose it will be for the historians to evaluate the impact of the occupation. They may well decide that great opportunities were lost, and much more of lasting value could have been achieved. However, there were limitations to what we in the rank and file could achieve, and with the volatile state of affairs in the Zone it was not always easy to pursue a steady course. Probably attitudes and personalities counted as much as anything. Despite the blunders and inadequacies of the CCG as an organisation, there were a great many people who did what they could in their own way, sometimes unconsciously, to try to bring a little bit of order out of the chaos; a breath of sanity out of the lingering madness. For the much harassed Military Government there came, from time to time, welcome murmurs of appreciation, exemplified in a few lines from a book by a Hamburg author, Herr Werner, about the struggle to return to normality, and the blessed state of ordered daily living . . . . . "Only a few months have passed by since the cessation of war but with the generous support of the British Military Government during this short space of time a great deal has already been done towards giving back to the Hamburg people a regular and peaceable life."

The phoenix *was* helped to rise from the ashes, and in the process underwent a profound transformation.

For my part, and the feeling would not be easy to explain, I always derive a certain satisfaction from being able to say about that strange occupation . . . . "I was there."

To Dr. Michael Loxton
from
Sevjiana Mehose
August 1988